C000091264

In Arabia, We'd

Stephen Adly Guirgis

Methuen Drama

Published by Methuen Drama

1 3 5 7 9 10 8 6 4 2

First published in 2003 by
Methuen Publishing Limited

Copyright © Stephen Adly Guirgis 2003

The author has asserted his right under the Copyright, Designs
and Patents Act, 1988, to be identified as the author of this work.

A CIP catalogue record is available from the British Library.

ISBN 0 413 77329-9

Typeset by SX Composing DTP, Rayleigh, Essex

HAMPSTEAD THEATRE PRESENTS THE EUROPEAN PREMIERE OF

In Arabia, We'd All Be Kings
by Stephen Adly Guirgis

Cast (in alphabetical order)

Lenny **Daniel Cerqueira**
Chickie **Ashley Davies**
Jake **Sam Douglas**
Daisy **Evelyn Duah**
Skank **Tom Hardy**
Holy Roller **David Hinton**
Charlie **Gerald Lepkowski**
Greer / Rakim **Colin McFarlane**
Demaris **Celia Meiras**
Sammy **Garfield Morgan**
Miss Reyes **Debora Weston**
Vic / Carroll **Benedict Wong**

Director **Robert Delamere**
Designer **Jonathan Fensom**
Lighting **Paul Keogan**
Sound **John Leonard** for **Aura**

Production Manager **John Titcombe**
Technical Manager **David Tuff**
Company Stage Manager **Julie Issott**
Deputy Stage Manager **Nasarene Asghar**
Assistant Stage Manager **Helena Lane-Smith**
Chief Electrician **Greg Gould**
Deputy Chief Electrician **Chris Harris**
Assistant Electrician **Simon Williams**
Wardrobe Supervisor **Lisa Shanley**
Wardrobe Maintenance **Selina Wong**
Assistant Director **Debra Hauer**
Casting **Gary Davy & Danielle Roffe**
Casting Support **Katie Milton**
Press Representative **Charlotte Eilenberg**
                    charlotte.eilenberg@dsl.pipex.com

In Arabia, We'd All Be Kings was originally performed at Center Stage, New York on 23 June 1999.

This production was first performed at Hampstead Theatre on 24 April 2003.

thank you

Andy Edwards
Stephen Willems – Literary Manager of MCC Theater Company, New York
Adam Woodward

The Company

Stephen Adly Guirgis (playwright) is a long time member of New York City's LAByrinth Theatre Company. His latest play, **Our Lady of 121st Street**, is currently running to critical acclaim Off Broadway at NYC's Union Square Theatre. His previous play, **Jesus Hopped the A Train**, completed an Off Broadway run, won the Fringe First Award at the Edinburgh Festival, moved to the Donmar Warehouse, transferred to The Arts and received an Olivier Nomination for Best New Play. **In Arabia, We'd All Be Kings** was named one of the Ten Best Plays of 1999 by **Time Out NY** magazine.

All three plays were originally produced by LAByrinth and directed by Philip Seymour Hoffman. Other writing credits include: **The Sopranos, NYPD Blue,** David Milch's **Big Apple,** NBC's **UC: Undercover,** and an upcoming FX film about exonerated Death Row inmates. A former Violence Prevention Specialist and H.I.V. Educator in New York City prisons and schools, he continues to work on stage, film and television as an actor. He will play the co-lead in Belladonna Pictures' feature, **Jailbait,** which begins shooting this summer.

Daniel Cerqueira Lenny

Theatre includes: **Days of Hope** (Oxford Stage Company / Hampstead Theatre); **Sleeping Beauty, The People Downstairs, The Art of Random Whistling, Afore Night Come** (Young Vic); **Plasticine, Mountain Language, The Crutch, Cleansed, Attempts on Her Life** (Royal Court); **Meat** (Theatre Royal Plymouth); **Luminosity** (Royal Shakespeare Company); **Powderkeg** (Gate Theatre); **Aunt Dan and Lemon** (Almeida); **Anthony and Cleopatra** (Moving Theatre Company); **Crocodile Looking at Birds, Ten Years of Freedom** (Lyric Theatre Hammersmith); **Handsome, Handicapped and Hebrew** (Grove Theatre); **The Brave** (Bush Theatre); **Waking Beauty** (Arts Threshold);

Caledonian Road (White Bear) and **The Girl on the Sofa** (Shanbuenhe am Lehninerplatz for the Edinburgh International Festival).

Television includes: **Cruise of the Gods, Sunburn, City Central, Hot Dog Wars, Pirate Prince, I'm Alan Partridge** and **Spooks.**

Film includes: **Tube Tales, Mad Cows, Toy Boys, Saving Private Ryan** and **Valley Girls.**

Ashley Davies Chickie

Born in Pennsylvania, USA. Ashley trained at LAMDA.

Theatre includes: **Romeo and Juliet** (LAMDA / European Tour) and **Twelfth Night, A Midsummer Night's Dream** (Natural Perspectives Theatre Company).

Sam Douglas Jake

Sam Douglas was a member of the Actors Space in New York City under Alan Langdon (Circle in the Square). He has a BFA in Acting / Directing from Simpson College, Iowa, and the University of Oklahoma Drama School, USA.

Theatre in the US includes: **The Rimers of Eldritch, Lion in Winter, A Doll's House, Journey of the Fifth Horse, Romeo and Juliet, The National Health, Equus** and the world premiere of **Blood Wedding**. In the UK: **The Resistible Rise of Arturo Ui** (Crucible Theatre, Sheffield); **The Floating Light Bulb** (Nuffield Theatre, Southampton); **Overland** (Script Factory); **In Praise of Love** (West End); **Desire Under the Elms** (Greenwich Theatre); **A Streetcar Named Desire** (Newcastle Playhouse); **Edmund** (Royal Court) and **Johnny on a Spot, Sweet Bird of Youth, A Raisin in the Sun, The Darker Face of the Earth, A Streetcar Named Desire** (National Theatre).

Television in the UK includes: **The Painted Lady, Kavanagh QC, Goodnight Sweetheart, Unnatural Pursuits, Jeeves and Wooster, Dr Finlay, Bodyguards, Armando Ianucci Show, Once in a Lifetime, Adrian Mole: The Cappuccino Years, Dinner Date, The Quiet Conspiracy, Reykjavic** and **The Edward R Murrow Story**. In the US: **Wolverine, The Tenth Kingdom, The Dirty Dozen, Next Mission, Highlander, Lexx, The Equalizer, Dogboy, To Be the Best, Magic Moments, Dirty Dozen III** and **The Last Days of Patton**.

Films include: **Fifth Element, Batman, Eyes Wide Shut, Mission Impossible, Snatch, Hackers, The Dressmaker, Death Wish III, The American Way, The Fourth Protocol, Dreamchild, The Razor's Edge, Lords of Discipline, The Snatching of Bookie Bob, Al's Lads, Laguna, East of Harlem, Mexicano** and **Octane**.

Evelyn Duah Daisy

Theatre includes: **Death and the Kings Horseman** (Royal Exchange Theatre, Manchester).

Television includes: **Babyfather, Goodbye Mr Steadman, Holby City, The Bill, Eastenders, London's Burning, Wonderful You, Jack and Jeremy Show, Punt and Denis, It's A Girl, Red Nose of Courage Comic Strip, Fashion Challenge, Grange Hill, Hands Across the World, So You Think You've Got Trouble, Missing Finger, Lifeschool 'Listen To Me'** and **Houseparty**.

Film includes: **The Exorcist: In The Beginning, Sliding Doors, Crocodile Snap** and **Circus**.

Radio includes: **African Stories, Lost Boy, The Bob Champion Story** and **Friends**.

Tom Hardy Skank

Tom makes his professional theatre debut in **In Arabia, We'd All Be Kings.**

Television and film includes: **Band of Brothers, LD50, Dot the I, Nemesis, Deserters, Black Hawk Down** and **The Reckoning.**

David Hinton Holy Roller

Theatre includes: **The Merchant of Venice, The Winter's Tale, Waiting for Godot, Hamlet, The Wind in the Willows** (Compass Theatre Company); **The Alchemist** (Tokyo Globe / Compass Theatre Company); **A Man for All Seasons** (Liverpool Playhouse); **The Railway Children** (Duke's Theatre, Lancaster); **Veronica's Room** (The Ashcroft, Croydon / Palace Theatre, Westcliff); **This Happy Breed** (Marlowe Theatre, Canterbury); **Electra** (Shaw Theatre); **The Art of Success** (Man in the Moon); **The Herbal Bed** (RSC Tour); **The Memory of Water** (RSC Fringe) and **Twelfth Night, Jubilee, A Russian in the Woods** (RSC).

Television includes: **Back Home Again, The Burden, London's Burning, The Knock, The Bill** and **Out of Sight.**

Film includes: **Flap.**

Gerald Lepkowski Charlie

Gerald trained at the Western Australian Academy of Performing Arts.

Theatre includes: **Twelfth Night, A Doll's House, The Three Sisters, The Balcony, My Night With Reg, The Dutch Courtesan** (Melbourne Theatre Company); **The Sisters Rosensweig, Much Ado About Nothing** (Melbourne Theatre / Tour); **Closer** (Black Swan Theatre Company, Australia) and **Bread and Butter** (Southwark Playhouse).

Television includes: **Halifax FP, Mercury, The Damnation of Harvey McHugh, Correlli, Genie Down Under, State Coroner, Good Guys Bad Guys, Blue Heelers** (Australia); **Monarch of the Glen, The Bill, Randall & Hopkirk** and **2000 Acres of Sky.**

Film includes: **Last of the Ryans, Witchunt** (Australia). Gerald will be appearing in the forthcoming **Doctor Sleep, Sixteen Years of Alcohol, Mandancin** and **American Cousins.**

Colin McFarlane Greer / Rakim

Theatre includes: **No Way Out (Huis Clos),** also producer & director (Cochrane Theatre / Riverside Studios); **The Lover / The Collection** with Harold Pinter (Donmar Warehouse); Berkoff's **Coriolanus** (West Yorkshire Playhouse / Mermaid Theatre / Tour); **Fair Ladies at a Game of Playing Cards** (National Theatre); **Two Horsemen,** for which Colin received Time Out, Best Actor Award 1994 (The Gate / Bush Theatre); **Othello** (Ludlow Festival); **Don't Fool With Love** (Cheek By Jowl); **Flamingo** (The Gate); **Black Poppies** (Stratford East); **The Relapse, Macbeth** (Birmingham Rep); **Blood Knot, Our Day Out, A Midsummer Night's Dream** (Derby); **The Duchess of Malfi** (Contact Theatre, Manchester); **Lincoln Mysteries** (Lincoln / Oregon, USA); **Coriolanus** with Corin Redgrave, **Romeo and Juliet, Outbreak of God in Area 9** (Young Vic); **Serious Money** (Library); **Dr Faustus** (Oxford Stage Company); **Chester Mysteries** (Chester City Company); **Edward II** (Royal Exchange Theatre, Manchester); **Boys in the Band, One Flew Over the Cuckoo's Nest** (Swansea Grand) and **Othello** (Chester Gateway).

Television includes: **Strange, Doctors, Judge John Deed: series 2 & 3, Babyfather, Holby City, Murder In Mind, American Embassy, Randall and Hopkirk**

(Deceased), Whistleblower, Black Books, Ted & Ralph, Eastenders, Kiss Me Kate, The Fast Show, Thin Blue Line, Final Passage, Back Up, Class Act, Mr Bean, Blue Iris, Runaway Bay, Side by Side, Lenny Henry Show, Jeeves and Wooster, Virtual Murder, Blackheart the Pirate, Black Poppies, Dutch Girls, Bust, Dempsey and Makepeace, To Have and to Hold and **Everyman – Chilling Out.**

Voice overs: Colin is also the voice of numerous channels and products including ITV, Red Bull and Charmin Ultra.

Film includes: **Chunky Monkey, Sorted, The Criminal, The First Nine and a Half Weeks** and **The Final Passage.**

Cartoons include: **Bob the Builder, Dennis the Menace, Kings Beard, Captain Pugwash** and **Oscar's Orchestra.**

Radio: BBC Radio Rep 1990 – 1991. Numerous readings and radio plays include: **Julius Caesar, Measure for Measure, Lavender Song** and **Ben Hur.**

Celia Meiras Demaris

Celia trained at Rose Bruford College.

Theatre includes: **Hannah & Hanna** (UK Arts Tour, India / Company of Angels Tour / Edinburgh Festival); **Merlin the Magnificent** (Unicorn Theatre); **Caledonian Road** (Almeida); **The Tempest** (Nuffield Theatre, Southampton / Tour) and **The Sound Collector** (Quicksilver Touring).

Television includes: **Silent Witness** and

three series of **Extra! Extra!**

Film includes: **Dot the I** and **Day of the Sirens.**

Radio includes: **I Think I Could Live With Animals** (BBC Radio 4) and **Hannah and Hanna** (BBC World Service).

Garfield Morgan Sammy

Though best known as an actor, also works as a director. He was Director of Productions at the Marlowe Theatre in Canterbury in the late 1950's. Associate Director of the Northcott Theatre in Exeter 1976 to 1978. Associate Director of the Nottingham Playhouse 1978 to 1980.

In a career spanning more than fifty years, he has worked in Europe, America and Canada, as an actor and director in theatre, films and television.

Debora Weston Miss Reyes

Debora trained at Yale and Central School of Speech and Drama.

Theatre includes: **Up For Grabs, The Seven Year Itch, Popcorn, Chapter Two, Serious Money** (West End); **See How Beautiful I Am, A Maiden's Prayer** (Bush Theatre); **Stop Kiss, Sheherezade** (Soho Theatre); **Yiddish Trojan Women** (Soho Theatre at the Cockpit); **Far Above Rubies** (Tricycle); **Butterfly Kiss** (Almeida); **Etta Jenks** (Royal Court); **The Revenger's Tragedy** (Cambridge Theatre); **Brighton Beach Memoirs** (Salisbury Theatre) and **The Misanthrope** (Judith Anderson Theatre, New York).

Television includes: **Shadows, Under the Sun, Mike and Angelo, Mosley, Gobble, The Perfect Family, Signs and Wonders,** In Suspicious Circumstances, Nobody's Children, **Under the Hammer, Small Metal Jacket, The Big One, The Final Warning, Magic Moments, Coded Hostile, The Return of Sherlock Holmes, Poor Little Rich Girl, 7 Wonders of the World, The Brooklyn Bridge** and **Dalziel and Pascoe.**

Film includes: **Possession, The Virtuoso, Martha Meet Frank, Daniel and Lawrence, RPM, Loch Ness, A Kid In Arthur's Court, Dropping the Baby, Patriot Games, Kafka, Shining Through, Nightbreed** and **The Birthday Fish.**

Benedict Wong Vic / Carroll

Theatre includes: **Julius Caesar, Anthony and Cleopatra, The Merchant of Venice, The Honest Whore** (Shakespeare's Globe) and **The Letter** (Lyric Theatre Hammersmith).

Television includes: **State of Play, TLC, The Bill, 15 Storeys High, Look Around You, Arabian Nights, Breakout, Hong Kong Cracker, Supply and Demand, Pie in the Sky, Frank Stubbs, The Chief, Medics** and **Small Metal Jacket.**

Film includes: **Code 46, Dirty Pretty Things** (winner of The Evening Standard Award and South Bank Show Award for Best Film 2003), **Spygame, Wit** and **Kiss Kiss Bang Bang.**

Radio includes: **Six Geese A Laying, Bound Feet In Western Dress, Saying It With Flowers, The Monkey King, Footsteps in the Jungle, The Iguanodon, The Great River, Kai Mei Sauce** (BBC Radio 4) and **The Joy Luck Club** (BBC World Service).

Robert Delamere Director

Robert studied at Hull University. He is an Associate Director of Associated Capital Theatres.

Theatre includes: **Accidental Death of an Anarchist, In a Little World of Our Own** (Donmar Warehouse); **A Russian in the Woods** (RSC); **Force of Change** (Royal Court Jerwood Theatre Upstairs / Jerwood Theatre Downstairs); **The Playboy of the Western World, Les Liaisons Dangereuses, Popcorn** (Liverpool Everyman and Playhouse); **Pinocchio in Venice** (National Theatre of Craiova, Romania / UK tour); **Les Liaisons Dangereuses** (Teatro Nacional San Joao); **The Playboy of the Western World, Jane Eyre, The Crucible** (Crucible Sheffield); **Julius Caesar, What the Butler Saw, Tartuffe** (Royal Exchange); For the Foundry: **Happy Valley, The Knocky, Brothers of the Bush** (Liverpool Everyman); **Neverland** (as producer, Royal Court); **Peter and the Captain, The Inkwell, Buster Keaton's Spin, The Puppet Play of Don Cristobel** and **The Shoemaker's Wonderful Wife** (Ragazzi/BAC) and **When Five Years Pass** (BAC, Edinburgh Fringe First Award). As Staff Director for the National Theatre: **An Inspector Calls** (Olivier and Lyttleton / UK tour).

Opera includes: **San Giovanni Battista, I Giganti della Montagna** (Battignano Opera Festival, Italy).

Television includes: **Animating Harry, Brookside, Brookside Christmas Special 2000.**

Future projects include **The Modernists** by Jeff Noon at the Sheffield Crucible. Robert has also written **Gone 'til the Satellites Turn Again**, a new play for BBC Radio 3 to be broadcast in July.

Jonathan Fensom Designer

Jonathan is currently working on **Breakfast with Emma** for Shared Experience, **Duck** for Out of Joint, **Little Baby Nothing** for The Bush Theatre and **Small Family Business** for the West Yorkshire Playhouse.

Recent work includes: **Abigail's Party** (Hampstead Theatre / West End); **Little Shop Of Horrors** (West Yorkshire Playhouse); **My Night With Reg / Dealer's Choice** (Birmingham Rep); **After The Dance** (Oxford Stage Company) **Be My Baby** (Soho Theatre / Tour); **The Mentalists** (National Theatre) **So Long Life** (Theatre Royal Bath / Tour); **Hay Fever** (Oxford Stage Company / Tour); **Woyzeck** (Birmingham Opera / European Tour); **Spike** (Nuffield Theatre, Southampton); **Navy Pier, Stop Kiss, Angels & Saints, Season at the Pleasance** (Soho Theatre Company).

Other theatre includes: **The Rivals** (Northcott, Exeter); **Passing Places** (Derby Theatre / Greenwich Theatre); **Erpingham Camp** (Edinburgh Assembly Rooms / Tour); **Alarms & Excursions** (Producciones Alejandro Romay, Argentina); **Blithe Spirit, A Streetcar Named Desire, Richard III, Bouncers** (Mercury Theatre, Chichester); **East** (West End / Tour); **Backroom** (Bush Theatre); **Dangerous Corner, The Government Inspector** (Watermill, Newbury); **Immaculate Misconception** (New End Theatre); **Closer Than Ever** (Jermyn Street Theatre); **Schippel The Plumber** (Palace Theatre, Watford); **Take Away** (Lyric Hammersmith / Tour); **Richard III** (Pleasance / Tour) Ghetto (Riverside Studios); **Roots and Wings** (Sherman Theatre); **A Nightingale Sang** (Nuffied Theatre, Southampton); **Yusupov** (Sydmonton Festival); **The Importance of Being Earnest, Billy Liar, Wait Until Dark** (Salisbury Playhouse); **September Tide** (King's Head / Tour / West End). Jonathan was also Design Associate on Disney's **The Lion King** (New Amsterdam Theatre, Broadway).

Television and film includes: **tvSSFBM EHKL,** (Arena) and **Tomorrow La Scala** (BBC Films).

Paul Keogan Lighting

Paul is soon to be working on **She Stoops To Conquer** at the Abbey Theatre, Dublin, **The Wild Duck** at the Peacock Theatre, Dublin, and **Un Ballo In Maschera** for Opera Zuid.

Other theatre work includes: **Eden** (Arts Theatre / Abbey Theatre, Dublin); **The Tempest** (Plymouth Theatre / Tour); **Olga** (Traverse Theatre, Edingburgh); **Too Late for Logic** (King's Theatre, Edinburgh); **The Silver Tassie** (Almeida); **Bailegangáire, Da, That Was Then, Chair, Tartuffe, Down The Line, Mrs Warren's Profession, Cúirt An Mhéan Oíche, Melonfarmer, The Electrocution of Children, The Map Makers Sorrow, The Tempest** (Abbey Theatre / Peacock Theatre, Dublin); **Antigone** (Storytellers, Galway); **Gates Of Gold** (Gate, Dublin); **The Wishing Well** (Kilkenny Festival); **Quay West, The Massacre At Paris** (Bedrock, Dublin); **The Spirit of Annie Ross** (Druid Theatre);

Down Onto Blue, Danti-Dan and **Mrs Sweeney** (Rough Magic).

Opera includes: **The Makropulos Case** (Opera Zuid); **The Queen Of Spades, Andrea Chenier, The Silver Tassie, Flying Dutchman, Madam Butterfly, Lady Macbeth of Mtsensk, L'Elisit D'Amore, La Bohème, The Marriage Of Figaro** (Opera Ireland); **The Lighthouse** and **The Rake's Progress** (Opera Theatre Company, Dublin).

Dance includes: **When Once Is Never Enough, Straight With Curves, The Rite Of Spring, Seasons** (Cois Ceim Dance Company); **Ballads** (Cois Ceim at Jacobs Pillow Dance Festival, USA); **Without Hope Or Fear, Sweet, Beautiful Tomorrow** (Mandance); **Chimera** (Irish and Mexican Tours); **Territorial Claims** (Dagdha Dance Company) and **Samo** (Blok & Steel).

John Leonard for Aura Sound

John Leonard started working in theatre sound over thirty years ago and hasn't stopped yet. He has worked in theatres all over the world for many organisations and producers, including the Royal Shakespeare Company, where he was Head of Sound and an Associate Artist. He received a Drama Desk award for his work on **Medea** on Broadway, is the author of numerous articles and an acclaimed book on theatre sound design and was named Sound Designer of The Year at the 2002 Entertainment Technology Show in Las Vegas. John is Sound Consultant for the Almeida Theatre and a Director of Aura Sound Design Ltd. Previous work for Hampstead Theatre includes **After the Gods, The Good Samaritan** and **Peggy for You.**

Dominic Shovelton Music Composition

Dom has spent several years composing music for film, television and theatre. A trained cellist, he also indulges the bass, guitar and AppleMac computers.

His background of both classical training & a passion for electronic music & production has moulded his compositional influences. An advocate of the 'dark arts' of computer based sound composition combined with the organic and unique expression of live performance.

He continues to work with other artists as a songwriter & producer including – **Sancheta Farruque** (Nitin Sawney, Sting) **Aref Durvish** (Jeff Beck, John MacLaughlin) **Marque Gilmore** (drumFM) **Eric Appapoulay** (Daniel Bedingfield) **David McEwan** (almost everybody!) **Geoff Woolley** (Good Looking Records) within a production collective, creating new music with a broad spectrum of influences from around the world.

Hampstead Theatre opened in 1959 in the upstairs room of The Three Horseshoes pub on Heath Street in Hampstead village. James Roose-Evans, the founding Artistic Director, quickly established an eclectic and adventurous artistic policy which holds good to this day.

In 1962 the audience had grown too large for the Three Horseshoes and a 174 seater portacabin in Swiss Cottage, expected to last 10 years, became Hampstead Theatre's new home. This temporary building lasted 40 years until the new theatre, designed by Bennetts Associates, was opened in February 2003 on Eton Avenue.

"Hampstead Theatre pitches itself just right. It knows what it is about, it strikes the right balance between production and performance with clarity and elegance, and it is clever enough not to steal the show"
HUGH PEARMAN, SUNDAY TIMES

Commissioning Policy

Jenny Topper, the current Artistic Director's commissioning policy is built on three central principles: to encourage commissioned writers to identify lucidly and frankly their particular passions; to be courageous and original in their ideas; and to respond with ambition to the formal challenges of playwriting.

Each year we invite the most exciting writers around to write for us. At least half of these playwrights will be emerging writers who are just hitting their stride; writers who we believe are on the brink of establishing themselves as important new voices. We also ask mid-career and mature playwrights to write for us on topics which have become crucially important to them.

Supporting Hampstead Theatre

Become one of Hampstead Theatre's **Luminaries** and you will be giving vital support to all aspects of our work, not just the plays on stage, but its education work and audience development programme.

There are three levels of support and benefits starting at £250 a year.

Our **Luminaries** are:

Level 1
(£250 donation)
Regina Aukin
Deborah Buzan
Richard Curtis
Mr & Mrs Robert Freeman
Linda Goldman
Peter & Elaine Hallgarten
Lew Hodges
Dr Arnold Horwell
Patricia & Jerome Karet
Marmont Management
Trevor Phillips
Tamara & Michael Rabin
Barry Serjent
Louisa A Service
Lady Solti
Simon Stapely
Hugh Whitemore & Rohan McCulloch
Dr Adrian Whiteson
& Mrs Myrna Whiteson

Level 2
(£1000 – £450 membership fee;
£550 donation)
Dorothy & John Brook
Charles Caplin
Prof & Mrs C J Dickinson
The Mackintosh Foundation
Michael & Olivia Prior
Mr & Mrs Anthony Rosner

Level 3
(£2500 – £1000 membership fee;
£1500 donation)
Richard & Penny Peskin

Corporate Partners

Our new **Corporate Partners** scheme offers a flexible package of benefits for you to entertain your clients, promote your business objectives and take advantage of everything the new theatre has to offer.

For further information on becoming one of our **Luminaries** or a **Corporate Partner** please contact the Development Department on 020 7449 4160 or development@hampsteadtheatre.com

Education & Participation Programme

Since its inception in 1998, we have had over 58,000 attendances from writers and actors aged 5 to 85. Now based in **The Space**, a flexible performance area in the new theatre, local residents and schools are encouraged to make use of the Theatre's expertise and facilities through a number of different projects: **Ignite**, an extensive programme of education and community outreach projects; **The Heat and Light Company** – open to ages 13 – 18 and a thorough introduction to all the essential skills that make theatre; an adult writing and drama course, **Generator** – available to everyone over 18, whatever their experience or ability; and **Nova** – for first time writers aged 55+.

To find out more visit our **website**, talk to us on 020 7449 4165 or email education@hampsteadtheatre.com

Priority Supporters

With advance information and priority booking you can be the first to discover fresh and dynamic playwrights, and make the most of a whole range of discounts for just £12 a year. For more details call us on 020 7722 9301 or email info@hampsteadtheatre.com.

Cafébar

Open 9.00am to 11.00pm Monday to Saturday, the cafébar offers a generous selection of sandwiches, baguettes, warm paninis and salads.

Our new building is also an ideal venue for celebrations or conferences. For further details email conferencing@hampsteadtheatre.com or talk to us on 020 7449 4205.

Hampstead Theatre
Eton Avenue
Swiss Cottage
London
NW3 3EU

T 020 7449 4200
F 020 7449 4201
info@hampsteadtheatre.com

www.hampsteadtheatre.com
Box office 020 7722 9301

   Camden

Charity Registration No 218506
Company Registration No 707180
VAT No 230 3818 91

"A grand, new playhouse for the 21st century"

NICHOLAS DE JONGH

whatcchu askin me for?

whatcchu tellin me for?

born bad
by Debbie Tucker **Green**
29 April – 17 May

directed by **Kathy Burke**
WORLD PREMIERE

Dawta wants the family to talk. But they've never talked like this before.

a special relationship?

besotted. betrayal

US and THEM
by Tamsin Oglesby
22 May – 28 June

directed by **Jennie Darnell**
WORLD PREMIERE

An English and an American couple embark on an enchanted friendship in this comedy of transatlantic manners.

Open from 9.00 am until late
Monday to Saturday
theatre / cafébar / workshops

hampstead theatre

Eton Avenue ⊖ Swiss Cottage 020 7722 9301 www.hampsteadtheatre.com

DONMAR

CALIGULA

BY ALBERT CAMUS
IN A NEW TRANSLATION BY DAVID GREIG

In this passionate, poetic and darkly comic drama, a charismatic leader is given absolute freedom to challenge social convention in pursuit of personal obsession.

MICHAEL GRANDAGE directs MICHAEL SHEEN in the world premiere of this thrilling new translation by award-winning playwright DAVID GREIG, whose previous plays include the highly acclaimed *Victoria* at the RSC, and *Outlying Islands* at the Royal Court.

24 APRIL – 14 JUNE

020 7369 1732
www.donmarwarehouse.com

In Arabia, We'd All Be Kings

Characters

Lenny
Daisy
Skank
Sammy
Miss Reyes
Demaris
Jake
Vic
Rakim
Sal
Charlie
Chickie
Greer
Man 1
Man 2
Holy Roller
Carroll

Setting

The play is set in the Hell's Kitchen/Times Square neighborhood of mid to late 1990s New York City. Mayor Giuliani's gentrification (Disneyfication) of the area was in full effect.

Act One

Scene One

Monday 3 a.m. The bar.

Lenny (*to* **Skank**)   There's two kinds a peoples in this world: those who annoy the shit outta me, but not enough for me to actually beat them; and those that are so fuckin' annoying that even after I beat them, I still doan' feel no satisfaction 'cuz I can still feel them inside a me, like when you eat some bad shit, like some crazy Indian food, and it just stays in there! You can't even shit it out 'cuz it, it lingers! You hear what I'm sayin': Linger!

Daisy   I want my money, Lenny!

Lenny (*to* **Skank**)   Put it this way: if I was the Mayor, I'd make a law that stated that all people such as yourself, if you kill them, all you get is like a summons!

Skank   Listen, man –

Lenny   – One more thing: get your hand out the peanuts!

Skank   Hey, big guy man, I have a right –

Lenny   – You have a right?! You have no rights! I'm a put it like this –

Daisy   – Lenny –

Lenny (*to* **Daisy**)   Stick a clam in it!

Daisy   You stick a clam in it!

Lenny   I should stick a clam in it?! Lemme tell you this – (*To* **Skank**.) Hey!! You think I'm playin'? Eat a peanut! Go ahead, eat a peanut! Please eat a peanut with those filthy hands so I could decapitate them right off your wrists like a lawnmower. I'll go 'Whaa-chump'!, you'll be handless!

Daisy   Lenny –

Lenny   – And you too! I'll 'Whaa-chump' you, you'll be lipless! You'll be talkin' shit, people be saying, 'What Daisy talkin' about?', and they'll be like: 'I doan' know, bitch ain't got no lips'!

Daisy   Gimme my money, Lenny!

Lenny   Money? What chu talkin', money? (*To* **Skank**.) Where you going?

Skank   Jukebox.

Lenny   I'll allow you to play A7, E4, and (*to* **Daisy**) baby, what's that other one I like by that rock guy wit' the –

Daisy   Gimme my money!

Lenny (*to* **Skank**)   A7, E4, you play anything I doan' like, I'll beat you.

Skank   OK.

Daisy   Lenny –

Lenny (*to* **Skank**)   And wipe down the buttons after you press them. (*To* **Daisy**.) He prolly got the herps, right, baby? Where's the beer taker? (*Shouts.*) Yo, beer! . . . (*To himself.*) Irish motherfuckahs, they're either standing over you like vultures waiting for you to fuck up, or they're disappearin' to the bathroom like ghosts. (*To* **Daisy**.) Did he bring the paper with him?

Skank   . . . Uh . . . dude? You got any, like, a coupla quarters?

Lenny   What??!!

Skank   It's juss that . . . Never mind.

Skank *goes to jukebox.*

Lenny   Goddamn right, 'Never mind'! This ain't no Banco Popular, motherfuckah! (*To* **Daisy**.) Man thinks I'm a ATM! (*To* **Skank**.) I ain't no ATM!

Daisy   I coulda told him that.

Lenny   What chu mean by that?

Daisy   Lissen –

Lenny   What chu tryin' to instigate? Huh?

Daisy   You need to check yourself, Lenny!

Lenny   I need to check myself?

Daisy   You need to check your ass.

Lenny   Check my ass?

Daisy   Don't talk to me.

Lenny   You need to check your ass! You better check your ass, or your ass'll be checked for you!

Daisy   Please.

Lenny   You'll be checking your ass into St Claire's after I beat that ass, with your lip talkin' to me like that.

Daisy   You wanna try me?

Lenny   I'm the man. You not the man. I'm the man. Respect the man.

Daisy   Respect the man.

Lenny   Dass right. 'Respect the man, you respect yourself.'

Daisy   Don't talk that jail talk.

Lenny   Respect the man!

Daisy   You still locked up?

Lenny   Respect the man.

Daisy   Respect the man?

Lenny   Juss like that.

Daisy   'Respect the man.'

Lenny   End of story.

Daisy   Respect the fat, unemployed, lives wit' his momma, man.

Lenny   You're crossing the border, baby.

Daisy   Why doan' you cross the border, get your ass a job, stop leechin'.

Lenny   You know what a leech is? A leech is a vermin. Point-blank: you think I'm a species of vermin?

Daisy   I'm going to the Chinese –

Lenny   – How you going to Chinese without me?

Daisy   One time! Gimme my money or I'll call your PO right now: 'Lenny's in a bar, he hit me, he got the crack in his pocket.'

Lenny   Call him!

Daisy   Fine.

Lenny   Wait! . . . C'mon, let's go Chinese together, be friends.

Daisy   I doan' think you wanna test me.

Lenny   I'm hungry.

Daisy   Lenny!

Lenny   OK, OK. Here, take the money, bring me back a Kung Foo Platter, some ribs, coupla spring rolls –

Daisy   Later for you.

Lenny   Yo, what kinda Welcome Home is this?

Daisy   Welcome home? I been Welcoming your crusty ass home all week! You been welcomed. You want some more welcoming?

Lenny   I'm juss sayin' –

Daisy   You are welcome to buy your own cigarettes! You are welcome to pay for your own drinks –

Lenny   – You got a short memory 'cuz –

Daisy   You are welcome to buy the fuckin' paper and look for a damn job!

Lenny   Fine! Fine! You wanna steak dinner? C'mon, less go. I'm gonna buy you a steak dinner with a bottle a wine and a friggin' pecan pie with the pistachio ice cream. C'mon, less go.

Daisy   You ain't buyin' shit.

Lenny   I'll buy it. Whaddya want? A yacht? 'Cuz I'll buy you a yacht. You know why? 'Cuz I love you –

Daisy   PSSSssssss!

Lenny   Doan' you walk away from me! Hey! . . .

Daisy   What?

Pause.

Lenny   Save me a coupla chicken wing.

Daisy *turns away, goes to exit.*

Lenny   I'll see you when you come back . . . (*She exits.*) Daisy! . . . Heartless! She a heartless individual . . . Sammy! . . . Sammy, your wife fuck wit' you like dat?

Sammy, *a very old drunk, stirs.*

Sammy   . . . My wife?

Lenny   Yeah.

Sammy   She here?

Lenny   Nah, Sam.

Sammy   Good.

Lenny   Gladdis fucks with you?

Sammy   Gladdis?

Lenny   Your wife!

Sammy   My wife? . . . You mean Gladdis?

Lenny   Yeah. She fucks with you, right?

Sammy   Fifty years.

Lenny   Long time.

Sammy   Fifty-one years next month.

Lenny   But you love her, right? . . . Sammy? . . . Sammy?

Sammy   Huh?

Lenny   You love your wife?

Sammy   My wife?

Lenny   Yeah.

Sammy   My wife? . . . Fuck my wife!

Lenny   OK.

Pause.

Sammy   She here?

Lenny   No, Sammy.

Sammy   Good. Fuck her.

Lenny   Fuck Daisy too! Fuck them all, except my mother. Sammy, you know my mother, right?

Sammy   Fuck your mother!

Lenny   Sammy, take it easy . . . I'm talkin' about my moms. You know my moms, she come in sometimes, Marisol. You know Marisol, right, Sammy? Sammy?

Sammy   Marisol?

Lenny   Dass right.

Sammy   I like Marisol.

Lenny   Thank you.

Sammy   Everybody likes Marisol.

Lenny Did she ever make you her Pernil?

Sammy Marisol, she's good. I like Marisol.

Lenny She raised me.

Sammy I'll tell ya somethin' . . . My wife here?

Lenny Nah, Sammy.

Sammy Good. I used to know a Puerto Rican lady named Marisol, back when I was still drivin' the bus.

Lenny Yeah?

Sammy She had a big ass!

Lenny Yeah?

Sammy I like that.

Lenny Right.

Sammy Gladdis . . . Is she here?

Lenny No, Sam.

Sammy Gladdis got no ass to speak of. She got that Irish ass, looks like a saltine cracker.

Lenny She gotta flat ass?

Sammy Gladdis's ass and my ass, it's the same ass, exact same, but this lady, the señorita Marisol, she had a big ass.

Lenny Uh-huh.

Sammy I like that.

Pause.

Lenny Yeah. The thing wit' Daisy, is, like, she say, 'Why you live wit' your moms,' you know, like chumpin' me and shit, and I'm supposed ta juss take her abuse, 'cuz thass the word for it, it's fuckin' abuse. But what I would like ta say to her, but I can't 'cuz then it'd be like World War III, is, 'You live wit' my mothah too, bitch! At least I got a mothah to live wit'! You think I need you constantly reminding me that

I'm past thirty-five still livin' at home?' . . . Thing is,
Sammy, like, maybe you could . . . Sammy? . . . Sammy?

Sammy   I ate a bananna in 1969, thought it was an
avocado.

Lenny   Sam?

Sammy   Avocado . . .

Lenny   Sammy?

Skank *returns from jukebox.*

Skank   Um, Lenny?

Lenny   Stop it. (*To* **Sam**.) Sammy? . . . (*To himself.*) Drunks
. . . Useless . . .

Skank   Lenny –

Lenny (*to* **Skank**)   You still here? Beat it.

Skank   Listen, a, Lenny –

Lenny   Don't call me by my name, that's my name! I get
called by my name from those I choose to allow them the
privilege. Get outta here! Now!

Skank   I juss thought maybe you could pick the songs you
like, man, because, a, A7 and E4, there's nothing there, and
so, why don't you just pick the songs?

Lenny   I should pick the songs?

Skank   Yeah.

Lenny   I look like a DJ?

Skank   I don't know, but, I got some selections over there,
paid for, and, uh, maybe, I mean if you want, you could
play E12 'cuz a, fuck, did I say E12? I meant B12, it's a,
dag, what is her name? You know, she was a jazz singer, she
was a junkie? Dag, man, it's on the tip a my –

Lenny   Get the fuck outta here now!

Skank   You know what? We don't have to listen to music
'cuz, a, music . . . music, fuck music! Right? Fuckin' music
fuckin' sucks!

Lenny   Wass your name?

Skank   My name?

Lenny   You know what? I don't need to know your name,
I'm gonna give you a name. Your name is 'About to Get
Your Ass Kicked Fuckin' Skank'. You got that?

Skank   Hey, man, that's . . . I don't like that.

Lenny   You don't like that?

Skank   I mean, it's cool, I guess, but –

Lenny   Listen, Skank, it's time for you to go.

Skank   OK, OK, I'll just be quiet, OK?

Lenny   No.

Skank   I'll sit in the back.

Lenny   No.

Skank   See, man, the thing is, thing is I got a drink
coming, from the guy, the bartender, so, a, I'd like to just –

Lenny   Do you see a bartender?

Skank   Do I see a, no, but . . .

Lenny   Do you see this knife?

Skank   OK. I'm leaving.

He exits. A beat. He returns.

This is wrong, man, this is, I want my drink! My drink is
owed to me and I want it, and if you wanna fuckin' stab me,
than fuckin' stab! OK? I been stabbed before, I'll be stabbed
again, fuck it, man, stab!

Lenny *goes to stab him.*

Skank   Whoa! Whoa! Wait! I'm goin', I'm goin'!

Skank *exits again. A beat. He opens the door very slightly and whispers through the crack.*

Dude? Big guy? Whoa, whoa! Don't get up. Listen. I'm gonna wait out here. When the bartender comes back, I'm gonna get my buy back, guzzle it, and split. OK? OK? . . . Right, great, I'll be out here.

Skank *exits. A pause. The bar door opens.*

Lenny   That's it, death!

Miss Reyes *and* **Demaris** *enter.*

Lenny   Oh. Hi, Miss Reyes. Hi, Demaris.

Miss Reyes   Oh my God! When you got out, baby?!

Demaris   It's fuckin' pourin' out there.

Miss Reyes   Guttermouth!

Demaris   Chicken head!

Miss Reyes   If you want to drink on my check, you better reconsider that attitude.

Demaris   My hair's all fucked up!

Miss Reyes   Keep playin' games wit' me, see what happens. (*To* **Lenny**.) Whassamatter, Poppo, no hugs and kisses? Doan' be stingy, baby, give it up.

They embrace; **Lenny** *half-heartedly,* **Miss Reyes** *with gusto.*

Mira, Lenny, you lookin' good, Poppo. They feeded you good up there, eh?

Demaris   How come Daisy at the Chinese eatin' wit' dat nigga?

Lenny   What?

Demaris   What his name, 'Cheyenne'?

Lenny   Who is Cheyenne?

Demaris   He a nigga.

Miss Reyes   He is not! He's one of those Bible people, Poppo, you know, decent, nothing to worry.

Lenny   But, Miss Reyes, that's my lady!

Miss Reyes   Lissen, Poppo, I know she's your lady, but, a woman like Daisy, a little religion couldn't hurt.

Demaris   Look who's fuckin' talkin'.

Miss Reyes   If you ask me, you deserve better, Poppo, a man with thighs like you got.

Demaris   You're disgusting.

Miss Reyes   I'm just saying.

Demaris   Buy a dildo, Ma, it's cheaper.

Miss Reyes   Can you believe that she came from out of my uterus, Lenny?

Demaris   I wanna margarita, Ma.

Miss Reyes   You thirsty, Lenny?

Lenny   Yeah.

Miss Reyes   Well, we gonna take care a that! All you can drink, then, we gonna drink one more! Ay, where's the bartender, what's his name, the Irish?

Lenny   Thass what I wanna know.

Miss Reyes (*shouts*)   Excuse me, Mr Irish, you back there?!

Demaris   Less go to the other place, Ma.

Miss Reyes   They doan' cash my check there.

Demaris   So? Just blow them like you do when I'm not around.

Miss Reyes   Demaris!

Demaris   I'm juss playin'.

Miss Reyes   Lenny doesn't know that you're just playin'!

Demaris   I'm juss playin', Lenny, my mother's a virgin.

Miss Reyes   Where is this man? (*Shouts.*) Excuse me, please, you have customers out here waiting for ordering!

Demaris   I went to Spofford!

Lenny   Yeah?

Demaris   I fucked bitches up! Niggas try to play me, I jack them up too! I got a new hairstyle, but it's fucked up because a the rain.

Miss Reyes   Demaris, stop flirting.

Demaris   I ain't flirtin'!

Miss Reyes   How's my son doing up there, Lenny? He's OK?

Lenny   Yeah. You should, maybe, visit him.

Miss Reyes   Please. It's enough with my husband and my grandson.

Lenny   Mr Reyes is locked up? When's he get out?

Demaris   Two thousand and seven.

Lenny   Thass not so bad.

Miss Reyes   Please. My first man was a black, he got locked up. Then I had a Irish, they locked him up. Demaris's father was Italian, he's still locked up. Mr Reyes can stay locked up, for all I care. You know what I'm gonna do? The next time I marry a man, it's gonna be an Indian man with his own newsstand, something nice.

Demaris   I wanna fuckin' drink, Ma!

Miss Reyes   You juss asking for the belt tonight, aren't you?

Demaris   The belt? What are you, trippin'?

Lenny   Listen, why don't we go to Donnelly's, you could cash a check there.

Demaris   Donnelly's? That's *been* closed.

Lenny   They closed Donnelly's?

Miss Reyes   Two years ago.

Lenny   OK, what about we go to that old lady's joint on 54th –

Miss Reyes   – That's gone, baby.

Lenny   So, fine, we'll go to that Muggsy's, whaddya call it, Bar and Tap.

Miss Reyes   Muggsy died, they making a Disney something.

Lenny   Disney?

Miss Reyes   Ay, bendito, you been gone a while.

Lenny   I thought Disney was Florida?

Miss Reyes   Disney's spreading, just like the AIDS.

Pause.

Lenny   Hey, Demaris, how's Wilfred, I ain't seen him.

Demaris   You ain't seen him 'cuz he dead.

Lenny   He's dead?

Miss Reyes   Oh yeah. Mira, after he died, his mother, she got so depressed, she died. And then her husband and his brother, they went out one night, and they died – except they got killed.

Lenny   Which brother you talkin' about? Carlos?

Miss Reyes   Oh no, not Carlos, but he dead too.

Lenny   What?

Miss Reyes   Yeah. He was doing real good, too. He finished his treatment program, and he got, like, a good job, right? So, his job, right? He was working in a lavatory for science, but he wasn't a scientist or nothing, he was a custodian, but he liked the job 'cuz you know how he was always innerested in, like, the stars and mechanics? Anyway, he was happy, and proud, too. He was walking around like his old self, you remember?

Demaris   Macho man.

Miss Reyes   Four foot eleven in shoes, but he could carry himself, right?

Demaris   He was cute.

Miss Reyes   Anyways, he was cleaning up the lavatory one night and he decided to mop the walk-in cooler 'cuz he was going all out on this job.

Demaris   Mami, tell him why they got a cooler.

Miss Reyes   Because a dead brains!

Lenny   What?

Miss Reyes   They do experiments on dead brains to see how they could make research. But they gotta be cold, 'cuz I don't know why.

Demaris   So they could be fresher.

Miss Reyes   Anyway, Carlos, he opens the cooler, walks in, starts mopping, and then he dies.

Lenny   How did he die?

Miss Reyes   You see, earlier, Carlos walked into the lab and saw that somebody had left out a really big piece a dry ice, like a mini iceberg. So Carlos, being Carlos, sees the dry ice getting wasted, so he drags it into the cooler and forgets about it. Later, like, hours later, he returns to mop the cooler but the dry ice, it makes gas, you know . . .

Demaris   Carbon dioxides.

Miss Reyes   The cooler was filled up with carbon-oxides, which is poison. And invisible! But Carlos didn't know he was walkin' into poisons 'cuz it don't smell like nothing, so he just died.

Demaris   Nigga died.

Miss Reyes   The worst part too? He died on pay day!

Demaris   Thass so messed up!

Miss Reyes   They found the check in his pocket. He didn't even get to cash his first check.

Demaris   See what happens when you try to do the right thing?

Lenny   I . . . We, we used to play handball together. Me, Carlos, Figgy –

Demaris   Figgy dead too.

Lenny   What?

Demaris   Nah, I'm juss playin'. He at Riker's.

Miss Reyes   Oh! Do you remember Mikey the Cop?

Lenny   Dead?

Demaris   Nah, but he was was one of the cops who shot that black guy.

Lenny   Ya mean the black guy in the papers?

Miss Reyes   No, no, not that black guy. It was . . . – All I know, it was one of those black guys they shot (you know how they do?), like from a coupla months ago.

Demaris   It was longer than that.

Miss Reyes   Anyways, one of the black guys who the cops shot this year, that I can't remember which one, it was Mikey who shotted him.

Demaris   Thass why I got a gun, so I could shoot back.

Miss Reyes   Doan' get me started on that gun, Demaris! Lenny, do you think it's proper for a seventeen-years-old girl to carry a gun?

Lenny   I doan' know.

Demaris   Tell him about Lucy!

Lenny   Lissen: anything *good* happen while I was gone?

Miss Reyes   Sure! They got a two-dollah movie theatre! . . . But now it cost three-fifty.

Demaris   They closing it, Ma.

Miss Reyes   Don't say that!

Demaris   Serious. They gonna make a underground shopping mall.

Miss Reyes   Thass not true!

Demaris   Face it bitch, it's true.

Miss Reyes   Demaris, what I told you about calling me a bitch?

Demaris   I'm juss saying they closing the theatre, bitch.

Miss Reyes   Stop it! Juss stop it.

Lenny   Demaris, you wanna smack? The fuck is wrong wit' you?

Demaris   Excuse you??!!

Lenny   Someone need to spank your ass.

Demaris   All I said was they closing the theatre 'cuz they closing it, and she need to deal wit' that and get a fuckin' job so we could go to the regular fuckin' theatres like regular fuckin' peoples. They closing that motherfuckah down, alright?!

Miss Reyes   No way! I'm gonna make a complaint to Giuliani!

Demaris   He doan' give a fuck about you.

Miss Reyes   Stop with the language.

Demaris   He doan' give a fuck about any a us niggas.

Lenny   Demaris!

Miss Reyes   Ay, where is this bartender? This is not right!

Demaris   Why they want a old, ugly, alcoholic bitch in their theatre for anyway?

Miss Reyes *smacks* **Demaris**. **Demaris** *punches* **Miss Reyes**, *takes out her gun.*

Demaris   I'll kill you, bitch!

Miss Reyes   Demaris, stop!

Demaris   You don't raise your hand to me, bitch!

Lenny   Demaris!

Demaris   Those days are over, bitch, you got that?!

Miss Reyes   I got it, I got it.

Demaris   Fuckin' slut. (*To* **Lenny**.) The fuck you lookin' at?

Lenny   Thass your mother.

Demaris   That ain't my mother! Thass a old dried-up bitch think she can still beat me down. Thass a bitch down there.

Miss Reyes   Don't talk back to her, Lenny.

Demaris *kicks* **Miss Reyes**.

Lenny   Hey!

Demaris   The fuck you gonna do? You a bitch too.

Lenny   Excuse me?

Demaris *turns the gun on* **Lenny**.

Demaris   You deaf, bitch? . . . You gonna spank me now, Lenny? . . . Lemme ax you somethin': when you was upstate, you was suckin' mad dick, right?

Lenny   What?

Demaris   Niggas was wearin' out that ass, right? Say 'Right'!

Lenny   Demaris –

Demaris   Say 'Right'. They took your ass. 'Right'?

Lenny   Listen –

Demaris   You think I'm playin' wit' you?

Lenny   No –

Demaris   – So answer the fuckin' question. They raped you, right? Right?

Lenny   Demaris.

Demaris   Say it, bitch, say it!

Lenny   . . . Yes.

Demaris   Yes, what?

Lenny   What you said . . . They did.

Demaris   They fucked you?

Lenny   Demaris –

Demaris   – For real?

Lenny   Yeah, Demaris, for real.

Pause.

Demaris   Swear to God?

Lenny   Yeah.

Demaris   They fucked a big ape like you?!

Lenny   . . . I mean . . . I, I fought back . . . I . . .

Demaris   Oh my Gawd!

Lenny What?

Demaris Oh my God! You so stupid!

Lenny What?

Demaris I was juss playin'.

Lenny What?

Demaris I was juss playin' and you shit your pants like a bitch!

Miss Reyes Demaris!

Demaris (*to* **Miss Reyes**) You got something to say? (*To* **Lenny**.) You got raped, huh?

Lenny Demaris . . .

Demaris Doan' worry, I ain't tellin' nobody . . . You a bitch, though. Get up, Ma, less go.

Miss Reyes OK, baby.

Demaris Doan' forget to remind me to get the Pampers on the way home.

Miss Reyes Yes, honey . . . I'm sorry, Lenny. She not like this when she takes her medicat –

Demaris Shut your ass! (*To* **Lenny**.) . . . You know what, though? At least the man who put his dick in your ass wasn't family. (*To* **Miss Reyes**.) Less go, bitch. Less go get a margarita.

Miss Reyes Yes, baby.

Demaris Less go!

They exit. **Sammy** *is sleeping.* **Lenny** *is alone. A beat.*

Jake*, the owner, enters from the back, sees* **Sammy** *sleeping.*

Jake Hey! Hey, fuckin' Rip Van Winkle, wake up! Hey!

Sammy Huh?

Jake   Get the fuck outta here!

Sammy   Shkeckin, shiiber froo.

Jake   This ain't a fuckin' hotel, Get out, old man!! (*To*
Lenny.) This fuckin' bum, I should charge him a day rate.
(*To* **Sammy**.) Next time you come in here, I'm gonna
charge you $22.50 for the day, like the fuckin' Carlton
Arms! You got that, Father Time?

Sammy   . . . Your father –

Jake   – My father's dead, juss like you gonna be, any
fuckin' day now.

Sammy   This used to be a nice place.

Jake   Yeah, then you came in.

Sammy *rises, crosses to the exit.*

Sammy   When you talk, I laugh.

Jake   Well, laugh outside.

Sammy   I'm laughin'.

Sammy *exits,* **Skank** *enters.*

Skank   Hey, man.

Jake   Out!

Skank   Right.

Skank *exits.*

Lenny   Say, Jake, where the bartender?

Jake   I fired his ass.

Lenny   Good.

Jake   He's in the back, callin' Ireland, cryin'.

Lenny   I been tryin' to get a drink for –

Jake   Daisy Hernandez, you know her?

Lenny   Thass my girl.

Jake   Yeah? Take her mail. Tell her she can't get her mail here no more.

Lenny   Why not?

Jake   Making changes round here.

Lenny   Changes?

Jake   Thass right. This ain't gonna be a skeeve house no more.

Lenny   Yeah?

Jake   Dass right.

Lenny   Well, thass good. Those people, they destroy the atmosphere, right?

Jake (*to himself*)   Where's the friggin' key, damn it? . . .

Lenny   Lemme get a, lemme get a shot a 151.

Jake   Last call was twenty minutes ago.

Lenny   What?

Jake   Bar is closed.

Lenny   Yeah, but –

Jake   Bar is closed.

Lenny   Lemme juss –

Jake   Bar is closed.

Lenny   I know, but –

Jake   Bar is closed.

Lenny   Look –

Jake   Bar is closed.

Lenny   You know what? You got a attitude!

Jake   Also got a bar, and it's closed.

Scene Two

Monday morning, 9 a.m. An office on 37th Street.

Vic   Siddown, Mr . . .

Lenny   Lenny.

Vic   'Mr Lenny', have a seat.

Lenny   Yes, sir . . .

Vic   . . . Sit . . . That's some cologne you're wearing.

Lenny   Thanks, uh, you want some?

Vic   I think you got us both covered there, Lenny. Quick question: you been drinkin'?

Lenny   Uh . . .

Vic   It's OK.

Lenny   Long night, but –

Vic   It's OK. If Vic says, 'It's OK,' then, 'It's OK,' . . . OK?

Lenny   Um . . .

Vic   Say: 'OK'.

Lenny   OK.

Vic   If we find you drinkin' on the job, you're out on your ass though, OK?

Lenny   I wouldn't do that –

Vic   So, Mr Lenny, tell me: why do you want to be an On-Site Field Marketeer?

Lenny   Uh, I thought this job was for handin' out flyers.

Vic   It is.

Lenny   Oh.

Vic   But it's a lot more than that, Lenny. Lemme ask you somethin', Len: where do you see yourself in five years?

Lenny   Thass a . . . I see myself . . . You know what I see,
uh –

Vic   Lemme tell ya a little story, Len. Three years ago, I
was right where you are now.

Lenny   Yeah?

Vic   Worse. Times are tough, right?

Lenny   A little.

Vic   Not for me, Len, not any more, and I'll tell ya why:
they took my house, they took my wife, my kids, my car, all
the creature comforts, you know what they didn't take? . . .
Ask me what they didn't take!

Lenny   What –

Vic   My *initiative*, Len! A man with initiative, like yourself,
like me, they can't take that away. Tell me the truth: you
almost didn't come, right?

Lenny   It's true.

Vic   But you did come. Hey! They can send me all the
college grads and MBAs they want, you know what I say? I
say: 'Send me one man with initiative. I don't want "Yale",
fuck Yale! Give me one guy: School a Hard Knocks and
some fire in his eye.' You got that fire, Len?

Lenny   I do.

Vic   'Cuz if you don't, please, tell me now.

Lenny   Nah, I got it.

Vic   OK . . . The moustache, it goes. We like our
marketeers clean-shaven.

Lenny   My moustache?

Vic   Policy . . . Now, hypothetical question: how many
flyers you think you can hand out in ten hours?

Lenny   Uh, like a thousand?

Vic   Doesn't help me. You could hand out two thousand, three; you could toss half a them in a garbage –

Lenny   I wouldn't do that.

Vic   That's not the point. The point is: can you get the people up here? Can you get ten people per day to come up here, apply for a credit card?

Lenny   Credit card?

Vic   You wanna hand out Chinese takeout? That's across the street. You wanna make commissions? That's here. Every person you get up here, applies for a no-deposit, low-interest credit card, pays the fee, and gets accepted, that's five dollars in your pocket! Get ten people, that's fifty! Get twenty people, Len, you're lookin' at a hundred a day, and that's on top of your regular three bucks an hour!

Lenny   Three bucks an hour?

Vic   After training, yeah. Now, here's a piece a paper. I want you to write down the name, address, and phone number of twenty of your friends and family, anybody you know who's got bad credit.

Lenny   For what?

Vic   Every name you give me, it's like you've handed out a flyer. Anybody you know buys a credit card from us, five dollars in your pocket.

Lenny   You know what? I would prefer to just hand out the flyers . . . With my moustache still on, if that's possible.

Vic   . . . I'm sorry to hear that. Tell you what, why don't you give me a call next week?

Lenny   No, no, you don't understand. I could hand out the flyers, I'm good at that.

Vic   I'm sure you are. Call me next week.

Lenny   OK, look, I'll shave the moustache, it's not a problem.

Vic   Like I said –

Lenny   I see how they hand out those flyers on the street, most a those guys, they don't do it right, I watch them –

Vic   Lenny, I got another appointment coming in.

Lenny   All right, why don't you just give me back my application fee, and I'll take off.

Vic   Non-refundable.

Lenny   What?

Vic   Is this your signature?

Lenny   Hey! Juss gimme my fuckin' five dollahs back.

Vic (*into intercom*)   Ray? Get Rakim and Sal in here, we got a problem with an applicant.

Lenny   Who you think you playin' wit'? Gimme my fuckin' five dollahs!

Rakim *and* **Sal** *enter.*

Rakim   Problem?

Lenny   What is this, a mugging?

Vic   Show Lenny the lobby.

Scene Three

Monday, late morning. The bar.

Charlie   Have you got a eight?

Chickie   No.

Charlie   You're supposed to say 'Go Fish'.

Chickie   Oh.

Charlie   Have you gotta nine?

Chickie   No.

Charlie Chickie?!

Chickie What?

Charlie You gotta say, 'Go Fish'.

Chickie Oh.

Charlie So say it then.

Chickie Go Fish.

Charlie Your turn.

Chickie OK, um, do you have a nine?

Charlie Yeah.

Chickie I'll take that, thank you very much.

Charlie Wait a sec, Chickie. I just axed you do you gotta nine and you said no, so how come now you gotta nine?

Chickie I don't know.

Charlie You do too know!

Chickie No I don't.

Charlie If I ax you, do you got something and you got it, you gotta give it to me.

Chickie Why?

Charlie 'Cuz, that's the game, understand?

Chickie Yeah.

Charlie OK . . . You gotta jack?

Chickie No.

Charlie C'mon, Chickie, I know you gotta jack.

Chickie No.

Charlie Chickie, look me in my eye and tell me you ain't got no jack?

Chickie . . . Oh, OK, here.

Charlie   Thank you.

Chickie   You happy?

Charlie   Yeah, I'm very happy.

Chickie   You don't look happy.

Charlie   . . . It's your turn.

Chickie   I don't wanna play. I'm hungry.

Charlie   You wanna eat something?

Chickie   Yeah.

Charlie   Whaddya wanna eat?

Chickie   Fish! Shrimps!

Charlie   You can't eat shrimps for breakfast. Shrimps are for lunch or dinner, not breakfast.

Chickie   Can I eat lunch or dinner with you?

Charlie   If you want.

Chickie   OK.

Charlie   Breakfast is for Egg McMuffins and Chocolate Milk, maybe some cereals, or, like, if it's a Sunday or a special day, you could have Pancakes and Bacon or Waffles wit' Whip Cream, somethin' like that. Oh! You know what?

Chickie   What?

Charlie   You could have salmon for breakfast, that's a breakfast thing.

Chickie   What's salmon?

Charlie   Whaddya mean?

Chickie   I mean, what's salmon?

Charlie   You don't know what a salmon is?

Chickie   What is it?

Charlie   A salmon is a salmon. It's a pink fish.

Chickie   Is it good?

Charlie   I don't know, but it's a fish.

Chickie   How about pizza?

Charlie   A pizza's not a fish, Chickie.

Chickie   Duh!! I know that! I mean, how 'bout pizza? For breakfast?

Charlie   Pizza for breakfast?

Chickie   Yeah . . . Pleeeease???

Charlie   OK, pizza it is.

Chickie   From the Arab place, OK?

Charlie   The Arabs?!

Chickie   Please??

Charlie   OK, from the Arabs.

Chickie   Sometimes I think you're nicer than my boyfriend.

Charlie   I am nicer than your boyfriend.

Chickie   No you're not.

Pause.

Charlie   I gotta go wash some glasses. Here's some dough for the pizza.

Chickie   You gotta girlfriend, Charlie?

Charlie   . . . Yeah. I got five girlfriends.

Chickie   How come they never come around?

Charlie   'Cuz they doan' live here.

Chickie   Charlie? Do you think some time we could do something? I mean, not as girlfriend and boyfriend, but, like, the way we are now?

Charlie   Yeah, we could do that.

Chickie   Charlie?

Charlie   Yeah?

Chickie   How come you're so big but José kicked your ass, and Jimmy and Ra Ra, they kicked your ass too?

Charlie   I doan' know.

Chickie   And that guy Ronnie, and that crazy guy with the hat that time, they kicked your ass too. Even my boyfriend could prolly kick your ass.

Charlie   I don't think so.

Chickie   Everybody always kicks his ass too, but he's little. My boyfriend, he always says, 'If I was as big as that retard –'

Charlie   – What retard?

Chickie   . . . Not you! Someone else!

Charlie   Who?

Chickie   I doan' know.

Charlie   Lemme tell you something, Chickie . . . You ever watch the *Star Wars* movies?

Chickie   Yeah.

Charlie   You know what a Jedi Fighter is?

Chickie   No.

Charlie   Chickie, a Jedi Fighter is Hans Solo and Obi Wan Kenobi and those guys over there. Even Darth Vader, you know Darth Vader?

Chickie   Yeah.

Charlie   Even he was a Jedi Fighter, but he used his
powers for Bad, so now he gotta wear a mask and shit. Jedi
Fighters got powers, like, they could do anything, OK?

Chickie   Yeah.

Charlie   Ya understand?

Chickie   Yeah.

Charlie   OK. I'm gonna tell you something, Chickie . . .
Me, I'm a Jedi Fighter.

Chickie   Charlie?

Charlie   I'm serious, I got a Jedi name and everything.
And I got powers. A lot a powers, but I can't use them for
Bad, or else, I gotta wear a mask like Darth Vader, and I
doan' think that would fly too good in the city. I got Special
Powers, but, why am I gonna waste them on Jimmy and
José and Ra Ra and those guys? I can't take the risk to lose
my powers by accidentally doing Bad against those them.
But lemme tell you this: if me and you was to go out 'just as
friends', and somebody tried to mess wit' you or do you
harm, you better believe I would use all my Jedi Powers
against them, even if I had to cross the line against them
and do Bad to them, even if I had to wear a mask for the
rest a my life because a it. I wouldn't care, 'cuz you would
be protected and safe, and even if they took me to jail, I
would give you money first so you could go eat shrimps,
OK?

Chickie   . . . OK.

Charlie   . . . OK. Go get the pizza now.

Chickie   Charlie?

Charlie   Yeah?

Chickie   Do you think you could show my boyfriend how
to be a Jedi? Me and him, we're supposed to go to
Baltimore to see his friend Jon Seda, the TV and movie
actor, and maybe you could come too, and you could teach

him how to be a Jedi, and maybe Jon Seda, he might wanna be one too, but mostly, you could teach my boyfriend 'cuz he'd prolly be good like you if you taught him. Could you do that?

Charlie   I doan' know.

Chickie   Why not?

Charlie   'Cuz my doctor over there at the place, he said that to be a Jedi Fighter, you can't lie, steal, and you can't do drugs ever.

Chickie   Oh . . . I think I'll go get the pizza now.

Charlie   OK.

Chickie   You want three YooHoos to drink, right?

Charlie   Uh-huh.

Chickie   I'm gonna get a Diet Shasta, OK?

Charlie   Yeah.

Chickie   Can I get some gum for me and some of those little chocolate donuts for my boyfriend?

Charlie   OK.

Chickie   Have you seen my boyfriend today?

Charlie   Nah.

Chickie   OK.

Charlie   Chickie?

Chickie   What?

Charlie   . . . Nuttin'.

Chickie   OK.

Chickie *exits. A beat.*

Sammy   . . . Shoulda, shoulda.

Charlie   'Shoulda, shoulda', Sam?

Sammy   What you doan' tell 'em, even if they know, they still doan' know . . . 'cept if you doan' want them to know. If you doan' want them to know, then they know . . . they always know, 'cept if they doan' know, which is why you gotta tell 'em. Shoulda shoulda.

Charlie   Buy ya a drink, Sam?

Sammy   Shoulda, shoulda.

Scene Four

Monday night. The bar.

Greer   It was different then –

Skank   I get ya, man. You gettin' him, there, Chickie?

Chickie   He's talkin' about it was different then.

Greer   I got a friend. Franklin. I call him up Friday night, and this is important, it's Friday night, OK?

Skank   Friday night.

Greer   Not Monday, Friday! Oh! I need a drink. Barman! I'll have another, but, please, with a twist. This is not a twist, this is a wedge. Twist good, wedge bad, OK? You wanna drink?

Skank   Sure.

Greer   Barman, one for him.

Skank   How 'bout Chickie, can she have one too?

Greer   She looks a little young.

Chickie   People say I look young, but then, when they see me up close, they say I don't look so young as they thought I was before they saw me up close.

Greer   Right, fine, whatever, give her a drink. So anyway, I call up my friend Franklin: 'Franklin, it's been so long, blah, blah, blah, I miss you.' 'I miss you too.' 'We should get together.' 'I was just thinking of you.' 'La la la la la.' So I say, 'Where you going out tonight?' Now, lemme tell you something about Franklin. Back in the day, if you wanted a party, just look for Franklin, because, I don't care if it's the deadest night of the week, if you find Franklin, you are gonna find a party, and a damn good one too. I'm talkin' about the Funhouse, Peppermint Lounge, the old Danceteria, I'm talkin' 'bout the Limelight when the Limelight was the Limelight! Palladium, the Pyramid, I'm talkin' about Studio 54. I'm talkin' about doing blow with Mick Jagger and Miss Liza Minnelli till 8 a.m. in the back of the limo and someone's grabbin' on your 'you know what', and somebody's got someone's tongue in someone's somethin', and everyone's feelin' it, you hear what I'm sayin'?

Skank   It's a fuckin' party.

Greer   Lord have mercy, but it was. So I says to Franklin, I says, 'What chu doing tonight, girl?' He says – (I swear to God, if I'm lyin', I'm dyin') he says, 'Well, Greer, I'm making a pot a tea and watching *The Blue Lagoon*.' I says, '*Creature from the Blue Lagoon*?'. He says, 'No, Brooke Shields and Christopher Atkins *Blue Lagoon*'. I says, 'C'mon, girl, turn off that TV, let's do it like we used to'. He starts talkin' 'bout AA this, 'jogging' that, and do I wanna go to a 'meeting'. You hear what I'm sayin'?

Skank   That's rough, man.

Greer   Motherfuckah started talkin' 'bout 'The Lord'. You feelin' me?

Skank   Shit.

Greer   I mean, when a man start talkin' 'bout 'The Lord', well, I was raised Baptist, I have heard absolutely all I need to ever hear about the damn 'Lord'. You wanna talk to me about 'The Lord'? You better be the damn Lord – or else it's 'Get out a my kitchen, girl, 'cuz breakfast is definitely over'! I mean, am I wrong?

Skank   Nah, man, I'm –

Greer   Everybody I know, it's the same shit: AA, NA, DA, GA . . . Name any fuckin' 'A', I know a motherfuckah fallin' for it. You know they got a support group for people who think they gettin' too much sex? . . . I mean, please. Have you ever known a man – gay, straight, whatever – Have you ever had anybody, ever, come up to you talkin' about, 'Oh, man, I am getting just *too much* booty, and the more booty I get, the more miserable I am'? Nigger, please.

Skank   It's ridiculous.

Greer   It's depressing is what it is. Used to be, take work for example. Everybody could go out, have a good time. Now? Shit. These assholes I work with, all they wanna do is drink one lite beer or one faggot spritzer and go home and shave their damn bodies and pump iron and eat alfalfa sprouts and meditate and watch that damn Calista Flockart Skinny Bitch Show. You seen that show?

Skank   Fuck that show, man.

Greer   I'll tell you right now: I never saw that show and I never will! I got better things to do with my time than watch some skinny bitch being a skinny bitch. (Pardon my language, but that's how I feel.) And I don't need 'The Lord' to tell me how to feel, or what to watch, and Christopher Atkins not withstanding, I will eat a damn pussy before I stay home on *Friday night* makin' tea and watching the damn *Blue Lagoon*! I need a drink and I need a smoke 'cuz I'm workin' up a sweat here. What are you smokin'?

Skank   Lemme check. Chickie? What are we smokin'?

Chickie   We got, like, different kinds . . . No, wait. We don't got different kinds. We got two Viceroys, a Merits, and a Newport, but that's for me 'cuz that's my brand. We got four cigarettes.

Greer   What's her name?

Skank   Chickie.

Greer   Chickie, why don't you go out and pick us up a pack a Dunhills. (*To* **Skank**.) You like Dunhills?

Skank   Absolutely.

Greer   They're from England, you know.

Skank   Really?

Greer   Oh yes. All the best tobaccos, they come from England.

Skank   Right, yeah, I heard about that.

Greer   Here's ten dollars, Chickie.

Chickie   They cost ten dollars?

Greer   No. Bring me the change.

Chickie   OK.

Skank   Hey Chickie, pick up a coupla a those little chocolate donuts. You know those little chocolate donuts, they're like fifty-nine cents?

Chickie   The kind you like?

Skank   Yeah. Those kind. (*To* **Greer**.) Do you mind if she picks up a coupla –

Greer   Be my guest.

Chickie   Can I get a Jamaican beef patty? They cost a dollar, but he gives it to me for seventy-five.

Greer   Fine, fine. But please, be quick.

Chickie   OK.

Skank   Chickie?

Chickie   Yeah?

Skank   Pack a Kools.

Chickie   OK.

Skank   And a Chunky. (*To* **Greer**.) You like Chunky?

Greer   Sure.

Skank   Two Chunkies. (*To* **Greer**.) Should you give her more money?

Greer   She has enough.

Skank   Right.

Chickie (*to* **Skank**)   You wanna come?

Skank   Nah . . . Unless – Hey, man, you feel like some blow? I know where to get some dynamite blow.

Greer   Good stuff?

Skank   Good?! This shit is, gimme twenty dollars, I'll get us a nice bag, we'll party. You wanna party, man?

Greer   Maybe later.

Skank   Later? See, later, they might be sold out 'cuz this stuff is like, it's really great, it's, it's, it's from fuckin', fuckin', it's from –

Chickie   47th street.

Skank   No!! '47th street', listen to her. You know where it's from? It's from Peru, this shit. Peru-tian, man. Gimme thirty dollars, believe me, this coke, you do a coupla lines, you could lift a bus, man. Serious.

Greer   Why don't we let Chickie here get our cigarettes, we'll have another drink, and we'll talk about it?

Skank   You wanna talk about it?

Greer   Is that OK with you?

Skank   . . . Yeah, sure, of course.

Greer   Great, so, hurry back, Chunky.

Chickie   Chickie.

Greer   I'm sorry, I'm thinking about that Chunky. (*To* **Skank**.) Excellent idea, by the way.

Skank   What?

Greer   The Chunky.

Skank   Oh, yeah, Chunkies, they're great. Yeah. You know what's good?

Greer   What?

Chickie   So, you wanna come with me?

Greer   He's staying with me.

Skank   Yeah, baby. I'll be here.

Chickie   Oh . . . OK.

Chickie *exits.*

Greer   Barman! Another round, *s'il vous plaît*!

Skank   *S'il vous plaît*, huh?

Greer   It's French. Do you speak French?

Skank   Sometimes, yeah.

Pause.

Greer   So tell me what's good.

Skank   Huh?

Greer   You were saying . . .

Skank   Oh, yeah, right. About the Chunkies. What's good is, you go to a deli, right? And you order a large hot chocolate, but you tell them to stick a Chunky in the bottom, right?

Greer   I love, love, love, love chocolate.

Skank   Yeah. Then what you do is, you sprinkle a little blow in it and you mash up a coupla Percoset, and you stir that in too.

Greer   Oh my God! Then what?

Skank   You drink it.

Greer   With a straw? With a spoon? What?

Skank   I juss use my mouth.

Greer   I bet you do . . . Wow! . . . Just, 'Wow!'.

Skank   Breakfast a champions –

Greer   – Can I tell you something? No, I better not. I need a smoke. I need a smoke now.

Skank   Lemme ask Sammy. Sammy? . . . Sammy, got a smoke? (*To* **Greer**.) I'll just go through his pockets, he won't mind.

*He goes through **Sammy**'s pockets, finds a pack. **Sammy** grabs* **Skank***'s arm and stares at him vacantly.*

Hey there, Sammy, I was just lookin' for a –

Sammy   – Whaddya wanna do, hold my hand?

Skank   What?

Sammy   Pat McDonagh says you'll stop askin' for the money if I was to just hold your hand.

Skank   Sammy, it's me.

Sammy   I like whiskey, you like tea.

Skank   Sammy, man, hey, hello?

Sammy   I'm not Jimmy Stewart. Jimmy Stewart isn't Jimmy Stewart. You think Jimmy Stewart don't like a little ass with his biscuits?

Skank (*to* **Greer**)   Help me out, man.

Greer   Hey, mister! Can I buy you a drink?

Sammy Huh?

Sammy *releases* **Skank**.

Greer Barman, a drink for the gentleman.

Sammy Thanks.

Greer No problem.

Sammy . . . You seen my wife?

Greer I don't know your wife.

Sammy I didn't ask you do you know her; I say did you see her?

Skank We haven't seen her.

Sammy Good . . . You sure?

Skank Yeah, Sam.

Sammy Good. Fuck her.

Skank OK.

Sammy Don't marry a good woman.

Greer We won't.

Sammy Marry a bitch, you'll sleep better.

Pause.

Skank That old guy's got an iron grip –

Greer – What's your name?

Skank My name?

Greer Thass OK. I'm Greer.

Skank Hey, Greer.

Greer I'm in real estate. You think a location like this could make money?

Skank Huh? Yeah, definitely.

Greer   So, what do you do?

Skank   Me?

Greer   Actor?

Skank   I done some acting.

Greer   I thought you looked familiar.

Skank   Yeah. You saw *Superman 3*?

Greer   I think so.

Skank   I had an audition for that. What about *Gladiators*; you saw *Gladiators*, boxing movie?

Greer   You know what? Yes. I saw that.

Skank   OK, in the beginning, when the Spanish kid with the rat tail, when he starts fighting and he beats that white guy with the tattoo?

Greer   Yeah?

Skank   That's me, man.

Greer   Really?

Skank   Look, see, here's my tattoo. In real life, the scene, it was longer, but in the movie it was like, 'There I am, *boom*! I'm down!'. You know that show *Homicide*? The kid with the rat tail, he's on that show. He's a friend of mine. Jon Seda, man.

Greer   I don't know him, but, I bet you're a lot better than him.

Skank   Yeah, well, nah, he's a good guy. I'm supposed to go see him, me and Chickie, we're supposed to go for, like, a visit, but, like, you know, schedules and shit. You think you could gimme twenty dollars?

Greer   For what?

Skank   I'll come right back.

Greer   You'll come back?

Skank   I juss gotta pick up this prescription, over at the Rite Aid –

Greer   – Prescription?

Skank   Yeah, it's my aunt. She gotta disease, man, it's bad.

Greer   What kinda disease?

Skank   It's really bad, man. It's . . . a bad one.

Greer   Look, it's not that I don't trust you –

Skank   – Greer, man, I'll pay ya back. My friend, he's comin' by, he's supposed to be here, he got money, he owes me money, he's rich! Maybe you know him. Nic Cage, the actor?

Greer   Nic Cage is comin' here?

Skank   Yeah, man. We took a class together.

Greer   You're fuckin' cute, you know that?

Skank   Yeah?

Greer   With your bitchin' little body. Lemme see your abs.

Skank   Hey, man.

Greer   You want twenty dollars? Lemme see your abs.

Skank *lifts his shirt.*

Greer   Nice.

Skank   You like that?

Greer   Yeah.

Skank   I look good, right?

Greer   OK, I give you twenty dollars, what chu gonna give me?

Skank   Hey, man, I'm not takin' the money, I'm juss borrowing it. My friend's –

Greer   – Yeah, yeah, 'Nic Cage, sick aunt, suck my dick kiss my ass', OK? I give you twenty dollahs, what chu gonna give me?

Skank   Lissen, man –

Greer   – OK, good night.

Greer *goes to leave.*

Skank   Wait, wait, wait! Siddown!

Greer   Talk to me, girl.

Skank   . . . Shit, man! What happened to trust, dude? What happened to taking a man at his word?

Greer   I sat back down for this?

Skank   I'm juss sayin' –

Greer   – You think you the only piece a ass on this street? I'll walk out that door right now and I'll find Younger, Better Looking, and Better Abs.

Skank   So go then.

Greer   No. I'm gonna hear you out, 'cuz you got nice eyes. You got nice eyes, you know that?

Skank   You like my eyes?

Greer   Your eyes got tragedy in them.

Skank   Tragedy?

Greer   Tragedy's sexy . . . Talk to me, tragedy, do business with me.

Skank   OK . . . first of all, forget twenty dollahs, OK?

Greer   It's forgotten.

Skank   Sixty dollahs.

Greer   Sixty dollahs for what?

Skank   OK. Sixty dollahs, we go to the bathroom.

Greer   OK.

Skank   I do a little show.

Greer   What kinda show?

Skank   A sexy show.

Greer   Yeah?

Skank   I'll gyrate, I'll touch myself.

Greer   Speak English.

Skank   OK, I'll jerk off for you. You can jerk off too.

Greer   Sixty dollars so I could jerk myself off? I could do that at home for free watchin' the damn *Blue Lagoon*.

Skank   Yeah, but with me, you get me.

Greer   Can I touch you?

Skank   No.

Greer   You must be jokin'.

Skank   OK, you can touch me a little. My chest, my arms.

Greer   Your ass?

Skank   Sorry, man. You can't touch my ass.

Greer   Forget it then.

Skank   You wanna touch my ass? For eighty, you can touch it.

Greer   Eighty dollars to touch your ass?

Skank   I'm givin' you a competitive price.

Greer   For eighty dollars I'm entering that ass! For eighty dollars, that ass gonna hail me a cab home, tip the driver, and cook me breakfast in bed the next morning.

Skank   I don't think you're aware of the current marketplace –

Greer   – Lemme tell you something about the marketplace, girl –

Skank   – I'm not a girl –

Greer   – I'm sorry, baby –

Skank   – I'm not a baby and I am not a fuckin' girl! You wanna talk business, let's talk business! Eighty dollars.

Greer   You wanna talk business?

Skank   Thass what I'm sayin'.

Greer   I'm gonna put it like this: twenty dollars, we go into the bathroom, you suck my dick.

Skank   Suck your dick? Dude, you're outta your mind.

Greer   Is this a racial thing?

Skank   Fuck you, man.

Greer   Good night!

Skank   Look, uh, if you want a blow job, Chickie'll do that for you.

Greer   Chickie? What the hell I want with Chickie?

Skank   You wanna blow job, Chickie blows.

Greer   Chickie ain't comin' back.

Skank   Yeah she is.

Greer   How many crackheads you know, you give 'em a ten dollar bill, they gonna come back?

Skank   Look man, if I say Chickie's comin' back, then, she's comin' back.

Greer   We goin' to the bathroom or not?

Skank   Look –

Greer   – Good night!

Skank   Wait!

Greer   I said, 'Good night Sweet Prince, this show is over!'

Skank   Fuck!!!

Greer   . . . What?

Skank   Fuck!! . . . (*Pause.*) . . . OK, I'll do it.

Greer   You gonna do it?

Skank   Forty bucks, I'll jerk you off.

Greer   Twenty bucks.

Skank   Thirty-five bucks, I'll jerk you, you can touch my ass.

Greer   Twenty bucks.

Skank   Fuck, man. Thirty bucks, OK? Thirty. That's it. thirty.

Greer   Twenty bucks.

Skank   This is bullshit, man. You know who I am? You know where I been? I was in the army, man. I was in *Hamlet*! Fuckin' Hamlet! I did a commercial, man. I saved a kid once. I took a kid outta a burnin' crackhouse, risked my life! If I had money and someone needed it, I'd give it to him! I give money to people all the time! I let Chickie sell my last bag last week, my last bag. Do you know what that is to give someone your last fuckin' bag?! How many of these scumbags out here would do that, huh? You know why I did it, man? 'Cuz I got the human compassion, man! I got the love in me, I got love! Love! What you got, man? What the hell you got?

Greer   . . . I got twenty bucks. What chu gonna do?

Pause.

Skank   Let's go, man. Let's do it.

Greer   What're we gonna do?

Skank   What you want.

Greer   Look me in my eyes . . . You know what I want to do?

Skank   Just do it, OK? I doan' wanna hear it, I just wanna do it. Give the bartender five bucks, he'll keep the bathroom clear.

Greer   Fine.

Skank   You get fifteen minutes, man.

Greer   Doan' worry, baby. What I wanna do ain't gonna take but five.

Act Two

Scene One

Tuesday, early morning. 8th Avenue.

Chickie   You gotta smile.

Demaris   For what?

Chickie   Watch. Do like I do, OK? (*To a* **Man**.) 'Hey, baby!' (*To* **Demaris**.) You gotta be like that. Like you're a party waitin' to happen. (*To* **Man**.) 'Hey, baby!' (*To* **Demaris**.) Think about money.

Demaris   I'm a bank some 'Benji's' tonight!

Chickie   Yeah, that's better. You doin' better.

Demaris   Yeah?

Chickie   But smile, like you know a secret.

Demaris   Yeah. Yeah. I'm wid dat!

Chickie   That's good! (*To* **Man 1**.) 'Hey, baby.'

Man 1 (*to* **Demaris**)   I like that ass.

Demaris   Fuck you, bitch!!!

Man 1 *hurries off.*

Demaris   You bettah run, little punk ass bitch!! (*To* **Chickie**.) Oh, shit! You see dat nigga run?

Chickie   Demaris!

Demaris   I'm sorry.

Chickie   They're not supposed to be running away from us, Demaris.

Demaris   How you gonna let a man disrespect us like that?!

Chickie   You know what? I think this is a bad idea.

Demaris   I said I was sorry, Chickie.

Chickie   No. It's good that you're like that. It's just not good if you wanna make money.

Demaris   I wanna make money. I wanna make money for me and my baby.

Chickie   You mean your boyfriend?

Demaris   My boyfriend? Fuck that nigga! I'm talkin' 'bout my baby, my blood.

Chickie   You mean like a kid?

Demaris   You nevah seent my baby? Look, thass my baby, thass Evan. Thass a nice name, right?

Chickie   Oh! . . . He's . . . he's cute.

Demaris   Right?

Man 2   Hey there, ladies –

Demaris   Get the fuck out my face, you wanna get shot?

Man 2 *hurries off.*

Chickie   Demaris!

Demaris   He was tryin' to get all up in my face.

Chickie   Yeah? So?

Demaris   Dat don't sit wit' me.

Chickie   I'm sorry, Demaris, but I don't get from you that you have what it takes to trick.

Demaris   So teach me.

Chickie   I did teach you.

Demaris   So teach me again.

Chickie   Demaris, it's not the worst thing in the world to be not good at this. It's prolly a good thing.

Demaris   No it ain't.

Chickie   There's a lot a other things you could prolly do. Like . . . rob!

Demaris   Nah, 'cuz, they say if I get locked up again, they gonna take Evan from me.

Chickie   But you could get locked up doin' this.

Demaris   But I heard the cops is friendly.

Chickie   Sometimes.

Demaris   I need ta make some bank, Chickie. I need ta make a place that ain't my mothah's place. I need ta be a mothah to my kid. I need bank.

Chickie   Demaris –

Demaris   I'll do whatevah you say, and I won't curse out no more peoples. I ain't tryin' to come to you wrong, I'm juss axin' you as a friend.

Chickie   As a friend?

Demaris   What are you sayin', that you ain't my friend?

Chickie   Demaris, you pulled a gun on me, that's the only reason I'm doin' this.

Demaris   So then, what? You don't like me?

Chickie   You pulled a gun on me!

Demaris   I was juss playin', Chickie, I wouldn't have shotted you or nuthin'.

Chickie   That's not what you said before.

Demaris   OK, so I apologize, OK?

Chickie   Demaris –

Demaris   Here. Take my gun . . . nah for real, take it. I got my initials on there, see?

Chickie   Yeah.

Demaris   Thass cool, right? You could keep it, like, as a gift. You to me . . . You like my coat?

Chickie   Yeah

Demaris   Try it on.

Chickie   Demaris –

Demaris   Juss try it on. It's nice, right?

Chickie   Yeah.

Demaris   Dass 'cuz it's Name Brand!

Chickie   It's furry inside.

Demaris   You could have it, OK?

Chickie   You mean, like 'have it' have it?

Demaris   . . . Lissen, mama, . . . I'm sorry about, like, threatenin' your life and shit. OK?

Chickie   OK.

Demaris   Dat ain't me. I mean, it is me, but . . . you know the dilly, right?

Chickie   It's OK, Demaris.

Demaris   So you could teach me now?

Chickie   I just really need to get high, you know?

Demaris   You could take my chain and pawn it. Here, take it.

Chickie   Do I have ta pay you back?

Demaris   Are you my friend?

Chickie   Yeah –

Demaris   – Then you doan' haveta! We friends now, OK?

Chickie   OK.

Demaris   We niggas, right?

Chickie   Yeah.

Demaris   And if a nigga's my friend, Chickie, then I got
that nigga's back. I want you to know that. And even
though you ain't really down, I still consider you as down,
'cuz you good people, you a friend. And if a nigga's a friend,
then I put them in the books for life. I put them ahead a
everybody, even family, 'cuz they the real family, know
what I'm sayin', Chickie?

Pause.

Chickie   Do you know who Jon Seda is?

Demaris   You mean that fine nigga from TV?

Chickie   My boyfriend knows him.

Demaris   Yeah?

Chickie   I spoke to him on the phone one time, he sounds
just like on TV.

Demaris   He fine.

Chickie   Me and my boyfriend, we're gone leave here
soon and go be with Jon Seda.

Demaris   For real?

Chickie   Yup.

Demaris   I could come too?

Chickie   I gotta ask my boyfriend first, that is, if I can find
him, but, yeah, maybe.

Demaris   I could bring Evan?

Chickie   Yeah.

Demaris   Jon Seda got like a mansion, right?

Chickie   He's got a built-in pool!

Demaris   For real? We could swim in there?

Chickie   Thing is, we gotta save money, 'cuz, you know how guys are, they don't save good.

Demaris   How much you got saved?

Chickie   Right now? Nothin'. I mean, I had something saved before, but, I had to make an emergency purchase 'cuz, well, I ended up smoking it, but, like, if me and you teamed up, we could be on the road with my boyfriend and Evan prolly like in a month.

Demaris   I like the way that sounds, 'On the road'. You mean like in a car, right?

Chickie   Yeah.

Demaris   Mercedes?

Chickie   Or a Ford.

Demaris   'Built ta last', right? And we could drink champagne in the car and play games?

Chickie   Yeah. And we could stay in motels.

Demaris   Thass like a hotel, right?

Chickie   Do you like poems?

Demaris   . . . Yeah.

Chickie   We could make up some poems in the car, like, poems about things.

Demaris   And eat chocolate!

Chickie   I'm thinkin' that when we get to Jon Seda's –

Demaris   – I'm gonna fuck that nigga, watch!

Chickie   We could be like two couples.

Demaris   You seen Jon Seda's ass in *Primal Fear*? Dat shit is clean.

Chickie   You ever smoke crack?

Demaris   Nah . . . but don't tell nobody.

Chickie   See, the truth is, Demaris . . . you're really bad at this, but, if you smoke a little crack, it's gonna take the edge off your . . . edge . . . ya know?

Demaris   OK.

Chickie   Especially when you're just startin' out, like you. It helps.

Demaris   So less go get some.

Chickie   . . . I'm a crackhead, you know that, right? I'm a pretty good crackhead, but still . . .

Demaris   So? I still like you.

Chickie   But if you smoke crack, ya know, people get addicted.

Demaris   I won't.

Chickie   No, but you might . . .

Demaris   I swear ta God I won't get addicted.

Chickie   Well . . .

Demaris   C'mon, Chickie, please??

Chickie   Well, here's the only thing I'm thinkin': when we get to Jon Seda's, he's rich so he could send us to Betty Ford, and we could get clean and quit for real and then we'd be just healthy and tan all the time and hang out with my boyfriend and Jon Seda.

Demaris   Don Johnson goes to Betty Ford, right?

Chickie   I think so.

Demaris   Ah-ight, I'll go. Not to fuck him or nuttin', but juss to, like, hang out, smoke a blunt. Take a photo.

Chickie   OK.

Demaris   Lissen: gimme back the chain. I'll pawn it and pick up some rock, OK?

Chickie   I could go.

Demaris   Nah, but, my friend, he could sell it to me cheaper, we could get bettah value like that.

Chickie   OK.

Demaris   I'll be right back.

Chickie   OK.

Demaris   Wait for me.

Chickie   OK.

Demaris   You're gonna wait for me?

Chickie   Yup.

Demaris   I'll be right back.

Chickie   OK.

Demaris   You gonna wait for me, right?

Chickie   Uh-huh.

Demaris   You my nigga, Chickie.

Chickie   You too.

Demaris   I'll be back like in ten minutes, maybe.

Chickie   OK.

Demaris   You gonna be here when I get back, right?

Chickie   Yup.

Demaris   For real?

Chickie   Yes, Demaris, for real.

Demaris   Ah-ight.

Chickie   OK.

Demaris   Bye.

Chickie   Bye.

Demaris   I'll be right back.

Chickie   OK.

Demaris   Wait for me.

Demaris *exits.* **Chickie** *lights a cigarette, smokes.* **Holy Roller** *enters.*

Chickie   Hi, baby.

Holy Roller   Are you lost?

Chickie   Yeah.

Holy Roller   God loves the lost.

Chickie   Yeah?

Holy Roller   Yes, ma'am, He does.

Chickie   What about you, mister? You love the lost?

Holy Roller   Me?

Chickie   You a cop?

Holy Roller   No.

Chickie   You wanna go somewhere and save me?

Holy Roller   I . . .

Chickie   Uh-huh.

Holy Roller   . . . I got a room, coupla blocks.

Chickie   Hundred dollars. OK?

Holy Roller   OK.

Chickie   Money now, mister.

Holy Roller (*opens his wallet*)   Three hundred dollars. Does that buy the afternoon?

Chickie (*takes the money*)   Let's go.

Holy Roller   . . . Jesus himself laid down with whores and sinners, serpents and snakes, people like you.

Chickie   I like Jesus.

Holy Roller   . . . 'And the last shall be first.' What's your name?

Chickie   Barbara.

Holy Roller   You shall be first, Barbara. You shall be first.

Chickie   OK.

Scene Two

Tuesday afternoon. The bar.

Daisy   They threw out the jukebox?

Jake   Hey, they got CD jukeboxes now.

Daisy   But it sound better when you could hear the record scratching.

Jake   You people ruined that jukebox.

Daisy   Don't put me in wit' those other people.

Jake (*re: his slacks*)   This fuckin' stain! Goddamn Chinks, I'm gonna shove this suit up their ass! Twelve dollahs for dry cleaning, and look at this! I look like I pissed myself.

Daisy   Lemme take a look, baby.

Daisy *bends down to examine the crotch stain.*

Jake   Twelve dollahs! The fuck does he get off thinkin' he can charge twelve bucks? . . . Fuckin' Yuppie Chink Fuck! (*To* **Daisy**.) Hey, hey! Ease off! Not in front of the Walking Dead over there (*To* **Sam**.) Hey! Whistler's mother! When you finish suckin' on that ice, it's goodbye time.

Sammy   . . . The hobos, if ya gave them food, they'd put an 'X' wit' chalk on your stoop so's another hobo would know it. They'd put an 'X' –

Jake   – Yeah yeah, 'X' this. (*To* **Daisy**.) Jesus Christ, look at this, this is supposed to be my Florida suit.

Daisy   You ain't goin' to Florida.

Jake   Watch me!

Daisy   With your wife, right?

Jake   Daisy, how many times we gotta plough the same field? Yes, wit' my wife. I got a wife, at least for now. I leave my wife now, whaddya think happens? She takes everything, I end up on a park bench wit' you and your pals. Not me, sister, I got bigger fish to fry.

Daisy   What about me?

Jake   What about you?

Daisy   How you gonna act like that to me?

Jake   Lissen, toots, I'm in a state a aggravation here, OK?

Daisy   You ain't sensitive to my feelings, Jake.

Jake   OK, you know what? If I wanted someone wit' feelings, I'd get one who I could take out in public! How's that?! . . . Ya see what ya made me do? Ya see how ya made me stoop? I need a brawd's gonna bring me back up to my level, not drag me down to hers.

Daisy   It's like dat, huh?

Jake   Sweetheart, look, why can't we enjoy the time we got now?

Daisy   I'm tired a you threatenin' Florida on me.

Jake   I'm sorry, OK? Lissen to me now: I made a reservation at the place you like, the Sizzler, and I'll tell ya what: I'll reserve the room till noon tomorrow, OK? We'll stay up late, make fun of the pornos like we used ta, make a night a it . . . Whaddya say, peaches? . . . Say, you like the dress I got you?

Daisy   Do you like it?

Jake   Like it? I can't wait to rip it off you! Lemme go back, get the keys, make a call, be back in a sec.

Daisy   Whatever.

Jake   Have a drink if ya like.

Jake *exits to back. A beat.* **Daisy** *pours a drink.* **Lenny** *enters.*

Lenny   Hey, honey, I seen you through the window.

Daisy   Whaddya mean?

Lenny   Sittin' here wit' Sammy. (*To* **Sammy**.) Sam-my! *Que pasa?* (*To* **Daisy**.) Hey, thass a beautiful dress.

Daisy   Lenny –

Lenny   Don't say it! Hey, the mirror is gone.

Daisy   Yeah.

Lenny   I miss you; I would like ta tell dat to you.

Daisy   Look –

Lenny   Lissen, I gotta coupla dollahs from my moms, why doan' we get a coupla slices, go to that cheap movie theatre I been hearin' about?

Daisy   Lenny –

Lenny   Lissen, this ain't easy for me to say, but –

Jake *enters from the back.*

Jake   OK, peaches. Let's roll.

Lenny   Peaches?? (*To* **Daisy**.) What's, what's goin' on?

Daisy   Nuthin'.

Lenny   How come you two's dressed like that?

Daisy   Lenny, it's not what you think.

Lenny   Think? Think what?

Jake (*to* **Lenny**)   Hey, bozo, take a hike!

Lenny Who you callin' bozo?!

Jake Say it walkin', buddy.

Lenny Why don't you make me? (*To* **Daisy**.) Wha', what is this?

Daisy You've been gone six years, Lenny.

Lenny So?

Daisy So I gotta have a life too.

Lenny Yeah, but . . . Him?! Him??!!

Daisy I love him.

Lenny You love me.

Daisy I need a man, Lenny.

Jake Last warning, pal.

Lenny (*to* **Jake**) You shut up! Just, shut up! (*To* **Daisy**.) You sayin' I ain't a fuckin' man? Dat what you think a me?

Daisy I need a man, Lenny.

Jake All right, that's it.

Lenny (*to* **Jake**) Wait a second! (*To* **Daisy**.) You want a man? I'll show you a man! I'm gonna get a job, and some money, and we gonna, we gonna go out! I'm a take you for a steak dinner and, and, then we gonna see a show; and I'm a take you on a horse and buggy through Central Park wit' a blanket ta keep us warm! Then, when we back together, I'm a come back and put a bullet in this motherfuckah's head right here! Count on it!

Jake You wanna do it now?

Lenny Count on it!

Jake You ain't doin' shit.

Daisy Jake!

Jake   Big talk, zero action! You ain't gonna do a damn
thing. Why? 'Cuz you ain't shit! I seen thousands like you,
thirty years in this sewer! You know what you are? You're
garbage, pal. Loser garbage. Look at me! You should jump
in the friggin' Hudson, sink to the bottom wit' the rest of the
crap, ya pussy. Do decent people a favor. Get outta here!
Go! . . . (Jesus Christ, look at my suit, I swear ta God I'm
goin' to Florida!)

Daisy   Jake –

Jake   You people got some surprises in store. Peaches, get
me a little more club soda, eh?

Daisy   Jake, you hurt him.

Jake   And what? You didn't? Fuck this noise.

Jake *exits.*

Daisy   Jake! (*To* **Lenny**.) You mess up everything.

Daisy *runs out calling for* **Jake**. *A beat.*

Sammy   . . . They put an 'X' wit' the chalk, juss like that,
Gladdis . . . 'X'.

Scene Three

Tuesday night. 8th Avenue. **Demaris**, *alone and wasted.*

Demaris   Who wanna buy some pussy up in this
motherfuckah?! Who wanna work my middle tonight? . . .
Y'all a bunch a punk-ass bitches!! (*A man walks by.*) 'Scuse
me, sir. Sir! You wanna blaze my ass? . . . How 'bout I suck
your little tiny pinga. (*Man hurries off.*) Faggot! Little Punk! . .
. Shit . . . (*A woman walks by.*) 'Scuse me, bitch, you a lesbian?
You want a little choacha? (*Woman hurries off.*) S'matter,
bitch? You know you want it! (*A man walks by.*) The fuck you
lookin' at, nigga? You nevah saw no 'ho before? Go home ta
your mama, bitch!

Demaris *starts singing the Boys 2 Men song, 'Mama'. A beat. A man approaches.*

Carroll   You got a nice voice.

Demaris   Shut up, I'm singin'.

She sings a bit more, then stops abruptly.

Dat was Boys 2 Men.

Carroll   That was great.

Demaris   Hi.

Carroll   Hi.

Demaris   Um, hi.

Carroll   Whaddya doin'?

Demaris   Um, nothin', but, um, I'm smilin', I wish Chickie could see, I'm smilin', right?

Carroll   Yes you are.

Demaris   I got criticized earlier, before, for not smilin', but now, I'm smilin', right?

Carroll   Hey, you got me smilin' now.

Demaris   I got a good smile, right? Does it look like I know a secret or some shit?

Carroll   It looks pretty.

Demaris   Thank you, thass a nice compliment, uh . . .

Carroll   So, whaddya up to?

Demaris   Um, yeah, like, you cute and shit.

Carroll   Thank you.

Demaris   So, like, 'You wanna party?'.

Carroll   What kinda party?

Demaris   You know, like, fucking?

Carroll   Hey, you cut right to the chase, don't you?

Demaris   Yeah, I'm like that. So, you wanna fuck me?

Carroll   For free?

Demaris   No, stupid, not for free. Sorry, I didn't mean 'stupid' like that, I juss meant not the 'for free' part. You know what I'm sayin'? 'Cuz, like, I tell you right now, I could fuck like a motherfuckah, wear a nigga out, know I'm sayin'? You cute, though. I like the way you, yeah . . .

Carroll   So, how much?

Demaris   How much you wanna spend?

Carroll   I'm flexible.

Demaris   You bettah be flexible, 'cuz, I'll wear your ass out wit' like positions and shit –

Carroll   Name your price.

Demaris   Ah-ight . . . How 'bout a 'G'? Thousand dollars, you could have this ass, plus . . . plus . . . look! I got some crack. You smoke crack? And also I got a blunt somewhere, where it go? Here it is!! It's good too, chronic! One 'G', I'll get ya high and fuck ya dry . . . thass a rhyme! Look at my ass! Thass a ass right there! Thousand dollahs, you can have it! Whaddya say? You got a light?

Carroll   Sorry, sweetie.

Demaris   The fuck you doin'? Get ya hands off me, nigga!

Carroll   Hit me, it gets ugly quick.

Demaris   Fuck you, bitch! Ow, nigga! That hurts!

Carroll   Let's go.

Demaris   Lemme get my cigarette.

Carroll   I'll get you another in the precinct, how's that?

Demaris   Precinct?!

Carroll   What are you doin' out on a school night anyway?

Demaris   Please don't take me to no precinct, mistah.

Carroll   Better I should leave you out here so you could end up like that girl we found in the dumpster?

Demaris   But they gonna take my baby if you bust me.

Carroll   Maybe they should.

Demaris   Dat ain't right what you said, mister! Dat ain't right!

Carroll   C'mon, kid, this is like going to the doctor; we give ya a lollipop when it's all over.

Demaris   Hold up a minute!

Carroll   Pop Tarts and Apple Jacks at the station house, let's go.

Act Three

Scene One

Wednesday morning. The bar.

Daisy Hey, Charlie, how you doin'?

Charlie Good.

Daisy I could get a Bacardi?

Charlie Nah.

Daisy Charlie, I wasn't axing it like a question. Gimme a Bacardi.

Charlie I can't.

Daisy Why not?

Charlie It ain't twelve.

Daisy C'mon.

Charlie You know I can't serve before twelve.

Daisy What about Sammy there? He got a drink.

Charlie Yeah, but he's old.

Daisy So?

Charlie So, he's old. He could drop any minute, like this, he won't go thirsty.

Daisy Gimme a Bacardi in a coffee cup then.

Charlie You make my job hard, Daisy.

Daisy Yeah, well, it's a hard world.

Charlie *pours her a drink.*

Charlie Three dollars.

Daisy You could put it on a tab?

Charlie   No more tabs, Jake said.

Daisy   Why not?

Charlie   'Cuz he said it.

Daisy   But why?

Charlie   I ain't tellin'.

Daisy   Tellin' what?

Charlie   The thing I ain't tellin'.

Daisy   Lemme get another.

Charlie   You ain't paid for the first one.

Daisy   I bet if Chickie wanted one, you'd give her the whole bottle.

Charlie   No.

Daisy   'Cuz you like her.

Charlie   No.

Daisy   I'm gonna tell her!

Charlie   C'mon, Daisy.

Daisy   Lemme get a double then.

Charlie *pours a double.*

Charlie   I like you a lot better when you ain't like this.

Daisy   You seen Lenny?

Charlie   Nah.

Daisy   He didn't come home lass night.

Charlie   Maybe he got caught up.

Daisy   I guess. How 'bout Jake? You seen him?

Charlie   Not yet . . . Nine dollars.

Daisy   Charlie.

Charlie   C'mon, Daisy: three drinks, nine dollars.

Daisy   So, if I had three drinks, then where my free one at?

Charlie   You gotta pay for three to get one free.

Daisy   So lemme pay you in the back.

Charlie   Nah.

Daisy   You doan' wanna touch my titties?

Charlie   C'mon, Daisy.

Daisy   Wha? You doan' like my titties no more?

Charlie   Nah, Daisy. It ain't nuttin' against your titties.

Daisy   So, what is it?

Charlie   It's things. Things is changin'.

Daisy   What things?

Charlie   Besides that, it ain't right. It ain't right for, you know, it ain't right.

Daisy   You sayin' you better than me?

Charlie   Nah, Daisy. I ain't better than you and those people out there, they ain't better than us. Probably, I'll miss your titties. I like 'em.

Daisy   Why you gonna miss 'em, they ain't goin' nowhere?

Charlie   Forget it, Daisy. I'll juss put the money in the register myself.

Daisy   You don't got a pay for me! I pay my own way!

Charlie   So, then . . . ah, forget it.

Daisy   Here.

Charlie   What's this?

Daisy   It's a toaster.

Charlie   Where'd you get it?

Daisy   My friend gave it to me.

Charlie   What's it do?

Daisy   It makes toast, the fuck you think it does?

Charlie   I get my toast from the deli, Daisy.

Daisy   What's goin' on round here, Charlie?

Charlie   Nuttin'.

Daisy   You ain't my friend no more!

Charlie   I am too, Daisy.

Daisy   No you ain't.

Charlie   I am too!

Daisy   Fuckin' Lenny, fuckin' Jake, fuckin' you. Thass OK, though. I know who my friends is.

Pause.

Sammy   Gladdis!!

Charlie   Yeah, Sammy?

Sammy   More tea!

Charlie   You want beer tea or whiskey tea, Sammy? . . . Sammy?

Sammy   I'm talkin' about the day they moved the Dodgers outta Brooklyn . . .

Charlie   Talkin' to who?

Sammy   Spit shine. I got my first spit shine with the old man, spit shine, shot a whiskey, Roy Campanella . . . Campy . . .

Charlie   Thass good, Sam.

Sammy   Mickey Owen come on my bus, I wouldn't let him on.

Charlie   Yeah?

Sammy   I says, 'You think about what you done, Mick, you think about it'.

Daisy   Charlie, please, stop talkin' to that fool.

Sammy (*to* **Daisy**)   Huh?

Daisy   Ah, fuck . . . Hi, Sam.

Sammy   Marisol?

Daisy   Marisol?

Sammy (*to* **Charlie**)   My wife here?

Charlie   Nah, Sammy.

Sammy   If my wife was to come in here now, oh boy! . . . Oh boy!

Charlie   I got ya covered, Sammy.

Sammy   Ya do?

Charlie   I got lookouts on both sides a 43rd Street.

Sammy   You look beautiful, Marisol.

Daisy   Thank you.

Sammy   You look even more beautiful than I remember. How'd ya get so beautiful?

Daisy   I don't know, Sam.

Sammy   'It's better to light one up than to curse the darkness.' Remember that, Marisol?

Daisy   OK.

Sammy   You gotta nice shape, Marisol.

Daisy   Thank you.

Sammy   Don't tell my wife.

Charlie   We won't, Sam.

Sammy   You seen my wife?

Charlie   I think she's at the A and P.

Pause.

Sammy   She's not at the A and P, Charlie. (*To* **Daisy**.)
I'm gonna light a candle for ya, Marisol.

Daisy   OK.

Sammy   I gotta light a candle for Gladdis first, but then
I'm gonna light one for you 'cuz you're more beautiful than
I remembered.

Daisy   Thanks, Sam.

Sammy   And what I remembered was pretty good.
Beautiful . . . beautiful . . . I wish we lived in Arabia . . .

Daisy   What?

Sammy   Arabia . . . (*He drifts off.*)

Daisy   Charlie?

Charlie   Here, Daisy. One on me.

Greer *enters with a fashionable-looking gentleman.*

Greer (*talking to his friend*)   See the bar? It's genuine
antique oak from 1937, feel how sturdy, smooth? But fuck it,
I want it out a here. The fixtures are for shit, but look at the
moldings. Nice, right? They can stay, maybe. This wall's
coming down, and that(!), what do you call that thing?
Anyway, garbage! Oh, And they got a great bathroom in
the back . . . OK, the walls: lime! I want everything lime!
You wanna drink? (*To* **Charlie**.) Barman! Two Herrendura
frozen margaritas, light salt, heavy lime, make it with
Cointreau. (*To his friend.*) That's French, you know.

Charlie   Uh, we doan' make that, we ain't got it.

Greer (*to his friend*)   See what I mean? (*To* **Charlie**.) Fine,
fine. Two beers. Cold. You got cold beer?

Charlie   Yeah.

Greer   Good. And take down that soccer poster, whatever it is, it's hurting my eyes.

Sammy   In Arabia, you can have two wives. (*To* **Charlie**.) One for you and one for me. (*To* **Daisy**.) And one for you, Marisol. Beautiful.

Greer (*to his friends*)   I'm thinkin' about keepin' the ol' man. Put him in a tux, you know, for atmosphere?

Sammy   In Arabia, . . . we'd all be kings!

Scene Two

Wednesday night. A park bench near the West Side Highway. **Skank** *is nodding.* **Charlie** *enters holding a bag with a Darth Vader mask in it.*

Charlie   Wake up, fuckin' junkie! Wake up, skell!

Skank   Huh?

Charlie   You shoulda been there for her. You shoulda protected her!

Skank   Huh?

Charlie   They got her on a fuckin' table all cut up and naked, I was there. Where the fuck were you?! You were being a fuckin' lowlife piece a shit junkie, thass where you was!

Skank   Wha'?

Charlie   You ain't gonna live another day, thass for sure. Thass the least I could do, you fuckin' bastid!

He attacks **Skank**.

You think it's funny? You think this is a friggin' joke? I brung her shrimps! Dey wouldn't let me leave them wit' her, but at least I brung 'em! What did you bring? You didn't even bring your stinkin' junkie self!

Skank   . . . Who?

Charlie   I woulda protected her! Kept her safe! I wouldn't a let her be hookin' or nothin', I woulda helped her! . . . I shoulda helped her! I shoulda! . . . I –

He puts on his Darth Vader mask and takes out a knife.

I'm crossin' to another place. I'm crossin' it, and I'm takin' you wit' me. You didn't deserve her . . . You never deserved her! She was a princess! She was a Princess fuckin' Leia, thass who she was! . . . She was, she was . . .

He takes off the mask, drops the knife.

Charlie   I woulda made her a princess. An Arabian princess . . . She woulda . . . She, she woulda . . .

*He empties his money out of his pocket, a few coins and loose singles. He drops it near **Skank**'s hands. He spits.*

Charlie *exits.* **Skank** *is giggling and gurgling, oblivious.*

Scene Three

Dawn. A park bench near the West Side Highway. **Skank** *is drinking his hot chocolate. A beat.* **Lenny** *runs by with a purse.*

Lenny   You seen 5–0?

Skank   Huh?

Lenny   Cops. You seen cops?

Skank   Nah, man.

Lenny   I know you?

Skank   What?

Lenny   I know you, right? Gimme your hat.

Skank   Hey, man. I'm juss sittin' here.

Lenny   Gimme the hat.

Skank   Here, man.

Lenny   Switch jackets wit' me!

Skank   What're ya talkin' 'bout, 'jackets'?

Lenny   I got no time here, OK? Switch jackets.

Skank   I doan' think my jacket's gonna fit you, man, no offence.

Lenny   C'mon, quick!

Skank   OK, OK, . . . hey, this is a nice jacket man, thanks.

Lenny   It's temporary, doan' stink it up. Take this purse, hide it in your pants.

Skank   Look, man, I'm holding here, I'm not lookin' to get busted, this is my quiet time here, bro.

Lenny   Juss hide it!

Skank   Where I'm going to put it?

Lenny   Look man, put it in your ass, I doan' care. Make it disappear.

Skank   You should calm down, man.

Lenny   Doan' tell me –

Skank   – Here, bro, have a sip a this.

Lenny   Juss talk to me like you know me, like we been here for hours.

Skank   Have a sip, man. Go ahead. Here, take the comics, pretend you can read.

Lenny   I could read. (*He takes a sip.*) This shit is good, what is it?

Skank It's good, right?

Lenny Damn, this shit is good.

Skank I'm gonna get that shit copyrighted, make a million dollars!

Lenny You should.

Skank Hey, don't drink it all, save me some.

Lenny Juss a little more.

Skank OK . . . We could share it.

Lenny You made this shit?

Skank Yup.

Lenny It's very creamy.

Skank I know.

Lenny But it has a kick.

Skank I'm a creative person, I got skills like that.

Lenny You see cops?

Skank Nah . . . What'd you do, knock over a ol' lady?

Lenny She wasn't that old. She was big.

Skank Yeah?

Lenny Bigger than me. She punched me.

Skank Yeah?

Lenny Yeah. I was gonna punch her back, but, then I woulda felt guilty.

Skank How much money she got?

Lenny I doan' know. I juss ran.

Skank Wanna open it?

Lenny Hey! Chill!

Skank   I'm chill, man.

Lenny   I'm gonna take that money, buy my girl a steak dinner, shut her ass up! If I got anything left, I'm gonna get a gun, a big fuckin' Gat, so motherfuckahs know I ain't playin'.

Skank   Good idea.

Lenny   Yeah.

Pause.

Skank   Hey, you heard about Sammy?

Lenny   Sammy?

Skank   The old guy, Sammy?

Lenny   What about him?

Skank   He died in the bar last night.

Lenny   Really?

Skank   When he died, Jake and the bartender, they put him on the street, laid him out like a strip a bacon, man, before they called 911. They didn't want the cops fuckin' up business, plus, something about insurance.

Lenny   Thass fucked up.

Pause.

Skank   When I die man, I wanna die here, with the sound of the traffic on the highway puttin' me to sleep.

Lenny   Yeah?

Skank   I almost died here last week, but Chickie came by, woke me up.

Lenny   Chickie's your girl?

Skank   Yeah . . . I should go find her. She's, like, missing.

Lenny   So's mine.

Skank   Who? Your girl?

Lenny   I doan' wanna talk about it.

Pause.

Skank   A guy jerked off on my face the other night for twenty dollars, man. He came right in my eyes.

Lenny   Yeah?

Skank   Like I was nothin'.

Lenny   Yeah.

Skank   Twenty bucks.

Lenny   Thass OK . . . . At least you got twenty bucks, man.

Skank   Thass what I'm tryin' to tell myself.

Pause.

Lenny   Let's open this bag, man.

Skank   . . . Want me to go?

Lenny   . . . Why? You wanna go?

Skank   Nah, but, uh, if you want –

Lenny   Nah, man, stay . . . Stay . . . You can stay.

By the same author

Jesus Hopped the 'A' Train

Lightning Source UK Ltd.
Milton Keynes UK
UKOW06f0644050617
302691UK00008B/82/P